SHELF LAYOUTS

FOR MODEL RAILROADS

Iain Rice

KALMBACH BOOKS

Kalmbach Books
21027 Crossroads Circle
Waukesha, Wisconsin 53186
www.Kalmbach.com/Books

Published in 2009
13 12 11 10 09   2 3 4 5 6

Manufactured in the United States of America

ISBN: 978-0-89024-690-0

All photos by the author unless otherwise noted.
Front cover photo: Well-known British scenic modeler and photographer Barry Norman in
front of the author's "Trerise" shelf layout.
Back cover photo: The author's daughter, Elsa, helps set shelf tracks.

Publisher's Cataloging-In-Publication Data

Rice, Iain.
  Shelf layouts for model railroads / Iain Rice.

    p. : ill. ; cm.

  ISBN: 978-0-89024-690-0

1. Railroads--Models--Design and construction. I. Title.

TF197 .R48675 2009
625.1/9

Contents

CHAPTER ONE

Possibilities and problems

A Maine Central U18B eases a peddler freight over the short harbor trestle at Roque Bluffs, Maine. This scene on the author's shelf-format portable layout is less than 18" deep. The railroad was featured as a *Model Railroader* project layout in 2003.

According to my Cambridge Dictionary, a shelf is "a long flat board fixed horizontally, usually against a wall or inside a cupboard, so that objects can be stored on it."

The words long and flat should be sufficient to rouse the interest of any red-blooded model railroader as long, flat sites are always good news. In fact, the bald dictionary description sells the shelf somewhat short in model railroading terms, as it has to be neither flat nor fixed if we don't want it to be.

Custom-made, three-dimensional shelves incorporating all manner of miniature topography are perfectly possible, and if we support them from a wall-mounted track system, our shelves need no space-consuming supporting structure. Furthermore, they can be set at any height we require, be integrated with other shelves above and below (ideal for multi-decking and the support of lighting and dust protection), and can be readily adjusted or realigned. For construction or maintenance, our layout shelves can simply be arranged to be removed to the workbench when we want to work on them. Shelves on track, I reckon, are a good answer to many a modeler's prayer.

Shelves as layout sites do have limitations, of course. There are definite restrictions as to how wide you can practically make them, how much weight you can put on them and what sort of railroad subject you can house atop them. You wouldn't want to try putting a 20-track yard, a big roundhouse and turntable, or a helix on a shelf! But those are things that not every model railroad needs, and given that a lot of real railroads are built on width-restricted sites, there's still plenty of grist for the shelf-modeler's mill. It just needs a little head-scratching and lateral thinking to marry up your chosen railroad subject with the peculiarities of shelf format.

A matter of proportion

Unless you're content with a dead-straight single track and no scenery, any shelf much narrower than about six inches isn't going to be a lot of use to you in any scale. At the other extreme, unless you're closely related to an orangutan, shelves wider than 30 inches or so mounted at a good viewing height are likely to pose insuperable reach and access problems. Big, wide shelves are also apt to be unwieldy and difficult to support.

Over a good many years of building shelf railroads, I've found that two feet or so is usually about the practical maximum for width, with around a foot-and-a-half being the most comfortable compromise. And as always, picking the best compromise is the key

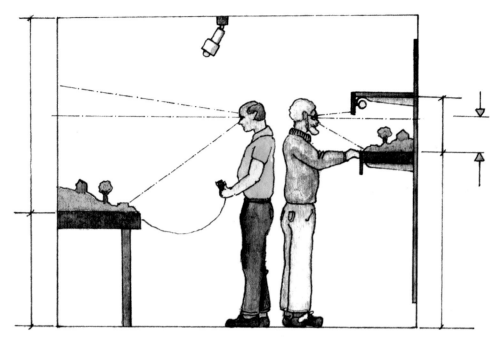

This shows the natural viewing angle of most people. Shelf layouts lend themselves to eye-level mounting, which puts the horizon line right where it should be. The top deck and valance permit efficient close-mounted lighting and create a shadow-box display. Traditional waist-level benchwork allows only a "helicopter view."

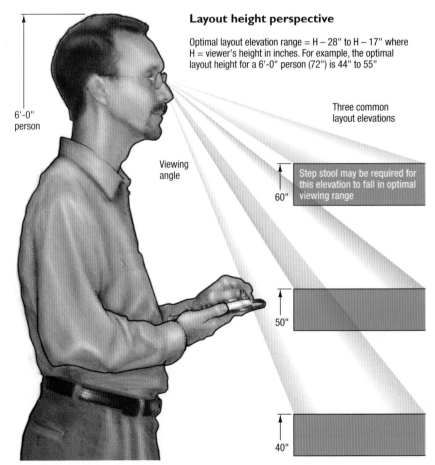

Layout height perspective

Optimal layout elevation range = H − 28" to H − 17" where H = viewer's height in inches. For example, the optimal layout height for a 6'-0" person (72") is 44" to 55"

6'-0" person

Viewing angle

Three common layout elevations

Step stool may be required for this elevation to fall in optimal viewing range
60"

50"

40"

Optimal layout height, shelf depth, and viewing angles vary depending upon the height of the operator, the number of decks, and the amount of clearance between decks.

to successful layout design. Rice's First Law of Model Railroading reads: "The man who never bowed to compromise never built a layout."

Available width is obviously a key factor in shelf layout design. But considering width in isolation is not helpful, as it is the proportions of a layout site—the width related to the length and height available—that really determine what you can accommodate, both practically and visually. For instance, there's no gain in pushing the width of a shelf site to include an eight-track classification yard if you don't have sufficient length for the necessary switching lead to service eight tracks.

The site shape also has to relate to the subject, or vice-versa. By and large, short-but-deep scenes are unsuited to shelves, while long narrow subjects are a natural. Fortunately, many aspects of

several railroad subjects come under those twin headings. The visual aesthetic of a shelf-based model is less obvious, but for a balanced scene pleasing to the eye, you do need to establish a good relationship not just between the width of the scene and its length, but also with the height.

Layout height

Height in this context has two interrelated components: scene height and display height. By scene height, I mean the distance between the lowest modelled point of the layout and whatever might restrict the view at the upper edge of the scene. There's no law that says that a model railroad—whether on a shelf or anyplace else—has to have a fixed scene height, at least until you hit the limit posed by the ceiling of the room in which it's sited.

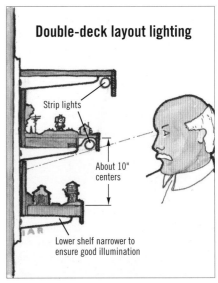

Double-deck layout lighting

Strip lights

About 10" centers

Lower shelf narrower to ensure good illumination

Effective lighting in multi-level layouts comes from fixtures mounted behind the fascia of the deck immediately above. The fascia hides the fixtures from direct view.

Many layouts don't have any form of top edge at all, relying on the limitations of our natural field of vision to cut out the "top of the sky" and other unnatural aspects or distractions around the upper edge of the scene. How well this approach works depends on a lot of things that have nothing to do with the actual model—things like the ceiling level, the height of the backdrop, the nature of the lighting, intrusions like overhead ductwork or piping, and the color and nature of the ceiling itself. And, most critical is the distance above floor level at which the layout is mounted.

One of the characteristics of a typically long-but-narrow shelf layout is that it lends itself most naturally to standing or walk-around operation, usually from quite close. That, in turn, calls for standing eye-level display, normally taken as having the track around 54" above the floor. The exact ideal height depends on your eye level and the nature of the layout subject. I'm a great fan of eye-level display as it both looks more natural and invites close-up viewing, which is a great incentive to go for better modeling standards.

Close-up viewing has another benefit. The nearer the distance from which you view a scene, the narrower your field of vision, especially in the vertical sense and consequently, the less height

The author's British-prototype "Trerice" layout is mounted with tracks 54" above the floor. The horizon line of the backscene is right on eye level for a natural view.

Model railroads based on logging railroads, such as Rayonier's Washington lines, will concentrate on scenery rather than structures. It's possible to capture the look and feel of this rugged topography on a fairly narrow shelf. *Stan Kistler*

you need for the scene to extend above your natural sight line. Taken together with the normally restricted depth (front-to-back) of a shelf-mounted model, this means that it typically need not occupy a great deal of vertical space—something that's often in short supply in a domestic setting.

It's in the nature of shelf-mounted layouts that they're often combined with domestic storage extending above the layout or come up against wall décor unsympathetic to the model. They also need lighting, which can be problematic. Relying on overhead room lighting is not usually an option, as you'll almost invariably be standing in your own shadow.

Shelf layouts nearly always demand a dedicated lighting set-up, introducing unwelcome and somewhat-visible hardware above the layout. Rather than take a chance on this lottery

of distractions, I'm a great believer in top-framing a layout by using an upper, high-level fascia or valance to define the top of the scene and to hide anything—lighting, wall décor, shelf supports, framing, and (especially) the upper edge of the backdrop—best left unseen. This upper fascia forms part of a top deck sited above the layout.

Top decks and shadow-boxes

A top deck is easy to contrive for a track-mounted shelf layout simply by using a second shelf mounted a suitable distance above that carrying the model. This "top slice to the sandwich" has a number of visual and practical functions. Firstly, it carries the all-important valance, which cuts off the vertical sight line to define the field of view and hide that great give-away, the top of the sky. Secondly, it supports, locates, and conceals the layout lighting

and cuts out distractions and intrusions from the room lighting—most notably, unwanted shadows.

This combination of functions is often termed a shadow-box display. The last important job of the top deck is to keep dust off the scenery and protect the model from things that fall from on high. With shelf-track layout support, adding this upper component is a cinch; it's simply supported from the same tracks using extra brackets, although it's usually better to suspend it beneath brackets as in the sketch rather than positioning the brackets conventionally, where they can show. Note also that the top deck needs to be a couple of inches deeper than the actual layout scene, so that light fixtures can be located far enough forward to properly illuminate the layout foreground.

The only tricky part in adding a top deck is positioning it correctly and

Modern industrial structures, such as this warehouse on Progressive Rail tracks in Lakeville, Minn., are low in height but big on footprint. This leads to sprawling track layouts that call for wider sites. *Jim Hediger*

deciding on the best depth for the fascia, factors that determine the viewing gap through which the layout is seen. Our natural field of view doesn't actually extend all that far upward when we're looking straight ahead, so for the fascia to function as a frame, it ideally needs to have its lower edge only a little way above our natural eye level. Usually, it should be no more than a couple of inches higher than eye level when we're standing in front of the layout at the normal operating distance of around two feet.

However, the cut-off sight line this produces will vary with the front-to-back depth of the scene, as shown in the diagram at the top of page 5. Since the elimination of the top of the sky is a primary function of the top deck fascia, then the greater the depth of scene, the taller the backdrop needed to get that sky edge up beyond the sight line. So a wider scene will typically call for a top deck mounted at a greater distance above the layout, with a relatively deep valance to chop the sight line in the right place.

All this sounds horribly complex, which it is in a theoretical sense, but theory never built much of a model railroad. In practical terms, a little experimenting with top shelf location and valance depth by mocking up the fascia with cardboard and thumbtacks will usually be enough to arrive at a suitable set-up for your particular case. Using adjustable shelf track to support the layout and top fascia/shelf makes this very easy to do.

You may well be surprised just how small the ideal viewing gap—the space between the layout and the lower edge of the top fascia—turns out to be. On my own eye-level mounted HO shelf layouts, mostly around a foot-and-a-half deep front-to-back, I've found 10 to 11 inches sufficient. Narrower shelves and smaller scales can work with as little as 8 inches.

The X factor

As will have become apparent, deciding on a good set of proportions for a layout shelf is, unfortunately, not a simple clear-cut mathematical business. I wish I could offer some magic formula that said "if a site is x inches long then the ideal shelf width is x divided by convenient constant, y, then the best height will be y + z." But, alas, there's no one right answer, as several different well-proportioned footprints are usually possible on any given site length.

What we also have to factor in is the X factor for the type of railroad and landscape that's going to sit on top of said footprint. As an example, let's consider a typical shelf site: a nice straight 12-foot-long wall devoid of any encumbrances. What shape of shelf and scene height would be best for 1) a modern-themed, industrial-zone switching railroad, 2) a traditional inner-city steam-era industrial switching district, or 3) a mountain-country logging line?

The key X factors to consider are scale, topography, structures and track layout. The influence of scale is obvious; the larger the scale, the bigger the objects in the scene and the more space—area and height—they'll take up. Topography mostly affects scene height. A hilly layout—such as the logger—may need more headroom to accommodate the different levels within the landscape.

Landscape features may also influence scene depth and the shape of the front edge-of-scene. Structures are a real crunch. If you've got big buildings, you need to ensure there's adequate footprint area and vertical space for them, although in the context of that cramped city scene, having the buildings extend out of the top of the scene, above the sight-line, can be effective at imparting the brick canyon feel. Using the valance shadow-box approach works well in this situation.

Track layout is both the most intractable yet the most easily adjusted aspect of the equation. It's intractable in that a given turnout will always need a given length. Curves must respect minimum radii, and clearance points cannot be ignored. Yet trackwork is easily adjusted because it's something over which we have total control and can readily alter.

Looking at our examples, we can apply the above criteria. The buildings of our contemporary industry zone would tend to be large, rectangular steel-span structures with a big ground footprint in relation to their height. Modern freight cars are also long, wide, and high and don't take kindly to over-tight curves, short spurs, and restricted clearances.

Trackage serving modern industries tends to be laid out for easy and convenient one-direction switching, keeping as much as possible to dedicated right-of-way. Modern track also has heavier rail, follows mostly straight alignments, and uses switches with fairly gentle frog angles. Contemporary industrial roadways are also wide and straight, while service aprons are laid out to allow plenty of space for forklifts and semi-trailers to maneuver.

Thus, industrial sites nowadays typically have an open layout based on a plain rectangular grid with the structures well spaced out. All of which would suggest the need for maximum footprint area but modest scene height. On our 12-foot site, a relatively wide shelf—say, a maximum of two feet with fairly constant depth—would be about right and would call for a backdrop around 15 inches high with a viewing gap of 10 inches or so.

In stark contrast, the older inner-city industrial area will be characterized by ultra-high density, with many tall-but-narrow buildings on all sorts of oddly shaped ground plans, packed together in a less than regular way. If ever there was a grid, it has long ago been forgotten and built over. Railroad right-of-way would be restricted, full of awkward jinks with tight, flange-squealing curves, and featuring predominantly street running.

Spurs—mostly able to handle only a few 40-foot cars—would shoot off every which way, squeezing through all manner of tight spots and calling for every type of cuss-awkward switching move. Track would be usually poor, with bad joints and kinks and lots of short-number turnouts. Much of the trackwork would be sunk in pavement, with little if any dedicated right of way. Maneuvering space for road vehicles would be equally tight.

To get that tall and crowded feel, the last thing you need is acres of baseboard real estate. In terms of shelf width, a foot would suffice and 15 inches would be plenty, with an outline to match the less-than-regular street pattern. Using the shadow-box approach, the scene height could be limited to somewhat less than the scale height of the structures, say, around 15 inches, with a 12-inch viewing gap.

The logging railroad is a different kind of animal. Typically, it'll call for a mere handful of structures, of which the only one with much of a footprint

Older industrial structures are taller, but often sit on smaller, irregular sites. These buildings are frequently crammed tightly together and served by street trackage. *Louis A. Marre*

would be a sawmill. But, unlike the other two subjects, it will involve plenty of topography. The right-of-way will be nebulous, tortuous and often vertiginous, winding in and out of trees and rocks and crossing chasms on spindly trestles. The track will go from bad to execrable. Spurs will be few, short, and mostly temporary. Most other railroad facilities will be absent, apart of course, from a gorgeous backwoods enginehouse.

The overall scene height will need to be enough to accommodate a sufficient slice of vertical scenery, although—like the brick canyons—there's no reason why the rocky sort can't extend off-scene vertically.

With the rise and fall of layout fascia typically associated with mountain scenery, the viewing gap between the straight upper fascia and contoured lower one will vary throughout the scene length.

As for the best footprint for such a layout, chances are it's probably going to be somewhat irregular, perhaps varying from nine or even six inches at the narrowest to 18 inches or more at the widest. But then, logging lines might be classed as extreme railroads, so the sort of benchwork they call for will surely be fairly far removed from the flat, rectangular slab usually associated with the word shelf.

Irregular shelves

Fortunately, shelves built for model railroads don't have to be simple square-edged slabs. There's no law that says they need be of constant width or depth throughout. In fact, I'd argue that in most cases, a shelf of varying width and thickness is highly desirable in opening up possibilities for scenery and track planning—as well as creating a more visually exciting presentation.

Those of you who have become familiar with my style of model railroad design will be aware that, when it comes to layout footprints, I'm a veritable curvy-outline fiend. I see no overall reason why shelf layouts should be deprived of the visual and spatial advantages of the curved scene edge, at least for the front of the layout. Given that most walls are straight, I'll grant you the desirability of following this basic alignment at the rear. That said, in some instances, the restrictions of the site or the need to match and integrate with non-layout shelving may dictate a straight and parallel front-age. The basic premise of my approach might be summarized as: "Just because it's a railroad built on a shelf it doesn't have to look like a shelf."

That's all well and good, but where does a curvy front edge leave width as a factor of proportion? The answer is as a mean value with regard to the length, although the scene height needs still to be related to the widest part of the scene. So a footprint varying in width between a foot and 18 inches would be regarded as having a mean width of 15 inches but would be set on a vertical spacing suited to 18 inches.

Some modelers argue that you should also vary the scene height with the width, but I've never been convinced by this. To me, the upper lighting fascia of a layout acts like a picture frame. It's an artificial boundary, and in this context, I find a straight line preferable to curves and consequent changes in level—and hence sight line—they bring. But I'm all for allowing an interesting shape that complements the scenic content and track plan of the layout.

Leaving aside the situation where the railroad must negotiate the corner of a room, the degree of curvature involved in the front of a shelf layout is generally going to be pretty subtle. I'm not suggesting wild swoops here, more like the gentle sinuosity of a slow-flowing creek. Given a basic mean width of shelf of, say, 18 inches for a 12-foot layout (a pretty typical value),

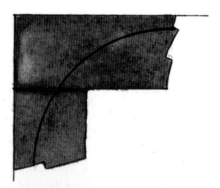

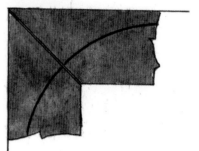

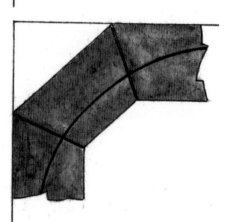

Shelves can butt together at corners; broad curves might require an angled connector.

then I'd be looking to vary the shelf width between about 16 and 20 inches to suit a typical railroad subject. Only for something as extreme as the logger would I consider any greater deviation from the average.

Multi-wall shelf layouts

If you're using more than one wall of a room to support a shelf layout, then you're going to have to get your track around a right-angled corner. This is a proposition that can offer problems or possibilities, depending on the type of subject you're modeling, the minimum track radius demanded by your equipment, and the mean width of your shelving.

There are two basic ways of supporting shelves around a room corner. You either run both shelves right into the corner so they meet at a butt joint of some sort, or you stop the main shelves short of the corner and link them with an angled corner shelf. With curves in the normal range of main line radii used for the various scales—say 18 inches in N scale, 30 inches in HO, and 60 inches for O scale—it's possible to get reasonable corner bends using a simple butted-together joint without ending up with awkwardly deep shelves. It's important to make as much use as possible of the shelf width by starting the curve from the rear of the scene. Only when you're using really narrow shelves or wider radius curves do you actually need to look at the angled corner board, although it will often offer better scenic possibilities.

I regard corners as a bonus as I've always preferred layouts that don't rely too much on straight lines in either track or scenery. Corners offer many opportunities for interesting scenic treatments and are no more of a problem on a shelf railroad than on a solid table-top or freestanding benchwork. Sure, they can pose minor practical problems with joint alignments and shelf support, but there is a range of solutions to these, described in the next chapter. The shelf railroad using two or more walls of a room can

often offer surprising lengths of run and a wide potential for interesting, visually separate scenes and multi-location operating potential even on a site shared with many other uses. There's no reason why you can't go right around a room, as crossing doorways, closets, and windows with lift-out links is not unduly difficult.

Lift-outs and linking sections

Thus far, I've been looking at shelf model railroads in the traditional form of a one-piece continuous scene, but this is far from the only possibility. I've had success with non-continuous footprints—layouts consisting of two or more completely separate self-contained scenes joined for operating purposes by linking non-scenic sections

Lightweight, non-scenicked lift-out sections work well for linking separate areas of a layout across windows or door openings. These sections can be straight or curved.

A classic Midwestern flat diamond (grade crossing) with both routes live is nearly impossible to model on a shelf-style model railroad. This junction scene is at Chippewa Falls, Wis.

that comprise nothing more than the bare roadbed and track with a safety fence down each side.

Such link pieces can be made straight or curved and can be designed to be left in place or made to lift out and be stowed when the railroad is not in use. They can be supported in a number of ways. They're effectively a bridge between the fixed parts of the layout, sitting on suitable pads at either end. However, they can also rest on brackets or shelf track fixed to walls, window or door frames, or they can sit atop furniture in the room conveniently located between the various parts of the layout.

Link sections can be made surprisingly light and robust. A roadbed of half-inch plywood cut to track width and fitted with a two- or three-inch-high fence glued and pinned down either side makes a rigid structure well able to carry the weight of a typical model train over a span of several feet without intermediate support. Links

can span doorways, windows, closets, beds, and other room fitments, and can often liberate room space otherwise unsuited to model railroading.

Gradients and multi-decks
A layout sitting on track-supported shelving is a natural for multi-decking. Supporting extra decks and lighting rafts is no problem and, with the vertical depth of the scenes being modest, the shelf format can facilitate two or even three decks in a surprisingly modest vertical space.

Using shelving or shelf benchwork designed to minimize the depth needed for the actual baseboarding means you can get two decks into considerably less than two feet and even three can be squeezed into under 30 inches.

Agreed, a 30-inch high three-deck layout may call for some form of step-up to view the uppermost scene and may require seated operation for the lowest, but in N scale, I've gotten away with three decks all viewed standing.

The deck heights were 46", 54", and 62" respectively. The total height of the three scenes—including upper lighting/dust protection over the topmost scene—was just 27", and the scenes averaged 9" deep.

It's all very well having shelves stacked to give two or more decks, but how do you get trains between them? The traditional method of linking multi-decks has been the helix, a space-hungry beast normally quite unsuited to shelf mounting and somewhat out of keeping with the compact style of plan normally associated with shelf layouts.

But there are other ways of getting trains between levels—train lifts of various sorts, variations on John Armstrong's ingenious vertical turnout (a form of see-saw for trains). Round-the-room shelving set at staggered heights permits a continuous grade between levels. Shelves themselves or non-scenic link sections can be set on a grade, although it's more usual to keep the shelf level and build the grade off

Triangular (wye) junctions are impossible to model on shelf layouts. This is the Rochester Southern at Rochester, N.Y. *Andrew Boyd*

it using roadbed and risers in conventional fashion.

The fact that we're only looking to gain 8" – 10" of elevation compared with the 15" or more called for by larger multi-deck layouts is a big help in contriving compact arrangements to link scenes. The high haulage power of many modern ready-to-run locomotives, coupled with the relatively modest train lengths typically found on compact shelf layouts, means we can use fairly steep grades to link scenes at different heights.

Expanding the scenic space

When you don't have a great deal of real estate for a model railroad, you need to make the most of what's available.

By their nature, shelf railroads tend to be tight in this regard and call for careful track planning to get in all the required features and facilities—a process that often results in the area available for scenery being squeezed.

Creating effective and realistic shelf scenes is usually all about maximizing the scenic potential of every available square inch—in which endeavor a backdrop is an absolute boon. All

scenic model railroads benefit from backdrops, but they are a key factor in creating spacious scenes on a shelf layout. How else can you represent thousands of acres in a few thousandths of an inch? With a good backdrop, even the narrowest of layouts can acquire a real feeling of depth and openness; in fact, at the extreme, you need little else.

The picture on page 6 shows my compact British-prototype portable shelf layout "Trerice." (Yes, there is such a place!) This tiny layout—it's roughly 15 x 56 inches—is packed with track and structures and thus has very little room for scenery.

The scene shown actually consists of no more than the track and a little vegetation either side of it—everything else is on the backdrop. Far from appearing cramped, the effect is surprisingly open and airy. The only limitation when using backdrops for tight scenes like this is making sure that the trains or other objects cast no unwanted shadows.

Backdrops are a fundamental component of shelf layouts and need planning in from the start. In addition to creating visual space and adding depth to the scene, they have a vital role in

cutting out distractions from the wall and the shelf-track system supporting the layout.

Colors suited to decorating walls often don't make a good background for models, while taped joints, patterned wallpapers, and shelf track definitely need hiding. The ideal for any backdrop is to create something that has a continuous surface free from sharp changes of direction, angles, and visible joints. I'll take a look at the practicalities of shelf backdrops in the next chapter.

Themes for shelf layouts

You can make some sort of a representation of almost any railroad theme—railroad type, geographical location, prototype road, or operating style—within the constraints of the shelf format. But to keep things practical, there are some features and locations you're probably never going to be able to fit on a shelf, while others are problematic and may need a little creative thinking.

In my experience, the most common no-nos are engine terminals featuring large roundhouses and/or long turntables, triangular junctions and turning

This scene was made for a shelf. Bridges can be long, but they are narrow. This is the Chicago & North Western at Chippewa Falls, Wis.

wyes, or flat crossings and interchanges at or near right angles with both routes live. But the vast majority of aspects of the prototype can be modeled in shelf format, and there are many common types of railroad scene or design element for which a shelf is every bit as well suited as a traditional table-top.

Chief among these are that most typical element of any railroad, the basic route-mileage right-of-way. Away from major features like yards, cities, junctions and crossings/interlocking plants, a railroad is essentially a very long, very narrow strip of land occupied by one or two tracks, the occasional drainage ditch, a fence or two, and a line of poles—a combination of features that can be readily represented on even the narrowest of shelves.

So suited is shelf format to representing such open country route mileage that even some of the largest basement-sited operating layouts—such as Bill Darnaby's Maumee Route and Tony Koester's Nickel Plate Road Frankfort Division—make extensive use of shelf systems for much of their main-line trackage.

Of course, I'm not suggesting that a compact shelf layout should consist merely of open-line trackage. However, even a quite modest shelf leaves room for passing sidings, spurs and loops, lineside industries, and a whole range of scenic features typical of what you'd encounter along the route of almost any railroad.

If you look at the footprint of a railroad on a map, you'll be struck by the fact that for the vast majority of the track mileage, the width occupied even by a busy main line is far less than a major highway. In fact, you could put the right-of-way of a trunk railroad up the median of the average Interstate!

Also, quite important stations and yards don't occupy much width in relation to their length. For most of the time, therefore, the proportions of a railroad are pretty well suited to those of a manageable shelf.

Of course, a modern scenic model railroad is about much more than merely squeezing in the trackage. The space demands of the scenic elements can all too easily conflict with trackage needs. Clever use of backdrops and low-relief modeling can go part of the way toward resolving this conflict, but truly sprawling prototypes are often incompatible with shelf modeling.

The portfolio of designs at the end of this book suggests ways of marrying up a variety of subjects with a shelf site. But just to round off this introductory look at shelf railroading, allow me to list a few thematic possibilities that strike me as ideal for modeling on a typically modest shelf site:
- Coal hauling through the narrow valleys of the Appalachians
- Almost any New England railroading this side of the New Haven main line
- Inner-city industrial, traction, terminal or streetcar lines
- Narrow-gauge mining lines in the Sierras
- Pretty much any logging railroad
- Most of the trackage that crisscrossed the prairie heartlands of the Midwest
- Mountain railroads with steep grades and near-vertical scenery
- Shortline railroading generally
- And, of course, my own favorite theme, harbor and waterside railroads

Only if you must have Tehachapi or the Keddie Wye is the shelf no use to you!

CHAPTER TWO

Practicalities

Anchoring a layout to a wall provides a clean, neat appearance and opens up space below the model railroad for storage. This is David Leider's HO scale layout, which has a 48" height and 36"-wide shelf. *David Popp*

The best shelves for building model railroads are generally those supported by a wall rather than being part of furniture or floor-standing units. Shelf railroads don't have to be heavy, so pretty much any wall will be sturdy enough.

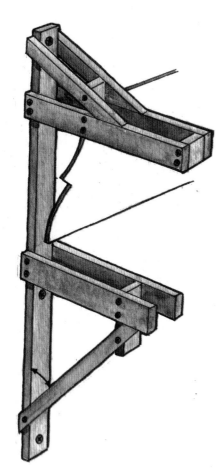

Traditional wood "gallows-style" shelf brackets can be made to suit a shelf format with an upper deck and lighting valance.

Shelf supporting systems

To support a shelf layout you can use individual brackets—either the commercial, pressed-steel kind or home-made wood gallows type—or some form of track shelf system using metal standards or track into which you place shelf brackets. In my experience, the track shelf is usually the simpler and quicker option. It spreads the load over a greater area of wall and, most importantly, it's adjustable, offering great flexibility in planning. I also find it easier to align and make plumb.

A single track upright can carry brackets for shelves above and below the layout, facilitating the addition of a top deck lighting/dust protection shelf, something I regard as an essential feature of any shelf layout.

The limitation of shelf track systems is the width of shelf they can handle, typically, little more than two feet. For wider wall-mount layouts, the gallows

bracket is a better bet. But even with gallows, I incorporate support for the upper shelf and lighting set-up, using the sturdy design shown in the drawing.

My preferred track choice is the double-hook-and-slot spur design, available in home improvement centers. Stick to one make, though; different brands usually aren't identical even if they look it! There are also some good single-slot tracks, which are fine where extreme strength is not required.

With track and brackets made in steel with a zinc or powder-coated color finish, track shelving systems typically offer shelves from around 6" up to 24" wide, the most useful sizes for model railroad use. These brackets are tapered, with the depth varying according to the length to make them rigid and stable under load. The locating slots are usually at a pitch of around an inch and a quarter, which gives a convenient step for height adjustment.

Given a strong enough wall, a good twin-slot track can take a loading of around 100 lbs. per bracket—so supporting the average model railroad is well within its capacity.

The channel-section steel track mounts by screws to wall studs or by wall plugs and screws into concrete or brick. You can buy the track in lengths from around two to six feet, and you can readily cut it with a normal metalworking hacksaw. Screw holes are provided at centers of around six inches, and it pays to use the largest-size screws that will fit—typically No. 10 countersunk. The actual length of screw needed depends upon the wall type and the load. For model railroading and normal domestic storage, I've found a 2" screw plenty long enough.

The spacing of wall tracks depends on a number of factors. Obviously, if you're attaching them to drywall, you'll need to be on top of studs if at all possible. Murphy's Law will say, of course, that there won't be a stud where you need to mount a track to support some key part of the railroad. In this case, you can install a screw-and-plug system designed to work in drywall sheeting. The sort of load you can put on these fasteners is nowhere near as much as on a stud, obviously, but they'll work

fine to support a layout. Bear in mind that each track upright only carries a part of the load.

How many tracks you use and the best centers for them depend to a certain extent on the layout design, but very often, other factors dictate track location. If the shelf track is only supporting the railroad, then you can space the tracks and arrange the benchwork sections to take best advantage of the situation. Where the track is also supporting shelving used for other purposes—such as bookshelves—then you'll need to take account of the loads and spacing of this subsidiary use.

And, of course, doors, windows, ducts, vents, and closets will all do their best to make sure you can't place a track where you want it! Fortunately, it's not difficult to arrange shelf layout benchwork to accommodate pretty much any feasible track placement in a given space, so long as you can arrange support somewhere near the ends of the various shelf sections.

The key thing when fixing shelf track uprights to support a model railroad is to get them truly vertical and placed accurately as to height. The essentials for this task are a long (four-foot or greater) spirit level, a good straight piece of lumber, and a willing pair of helping hands.

The important point about the height is that you need to fix the track so that the slots on each section of track are exactly level with one another, so that the brackets—and hence the

Several types of track shelving can be used for supporting a shelf layout. Stick with the same brand and style for the entire layout.

shelf itself—will sit level and true. I long ago learned the way you don't do this is to assume the floor is level and measure off that! Rather, you select one length of track as a reference point, fix that, then use shelf brackets, the straight piece of lumber, and the long spirit level to set all the other tracks to match it, as in the picture.

It pays to take great care over this, and you'll need that pair of helping hands to hold everything in place while you make the corrections. The more tracks you have to fix, the harder it is to get them all lined up—so for this reason, I generally try to use as few tracks as possible and design my benchwork to accommodate the resulting longer spans and joining centers.

The requirement for accurate vertical location is only really critical in terms of the track being exactly plumb in the plane of the wall, so that the top surfaces of the brackets will be level and they will all be truly parallel.

As with level floors, I've found that it never pays to assume that the walls are upright and flat. Invariably, each length of track will need careful checking with the long level used in plumb mode—usually followed by placement of a little packing here and there to get it absolutely vertical.

For packing, I use small pieces of sheet modeling wood, which is soft enough to be compressed slightly if need be when getting the track set true. For neatness of appearance, the tracks also need to be upright and parallel on the face of the wall, but a degree or two of error here isn't so critical.

Shelf benchwork

At the most basic level, a shelf layout can do without any benchwork other than the simple plank of a normal shelf. However, trying to build a realistic model railroad on a dead-flat rectangular slab of plastic-faced particle board is somewhat limiting.

Normal shelf boards are also less than ideal as a foundation for a railroad. They're prone to sag or twist, won't take pins or spikes, and don't leave you any place to run the wiring. You can make a form of subsidiary shelf work to sit on top of a regular

It's vital that the notches in the shelving tracks align in order to keep the shelf level. A straight 1 x 2 or 1 x 3 and a long spirit level work well for this. It helps to have an extra pair of hands (as here those of the author's daughter, Elsa) assisting in the installation process.

shelf, but if you're going to that much trouble, you may as well go the extra few yards and build some decent purpose-built shelf benchwork.

When it comes to benchwork of any kind, I'm a great believer in making it at least transportable, if not truly portable. That means robust, self-supporting, manageable-sized sections that aren't too heavy—qualities that are even more desirable in the context of a shelf layout. Why? Well, for a start, one of the virtues of track-supported shelf layouts is that they can easily move when you do, being quick to dismantle, leaving only a few screw-holes in the walls, and taking only a few hours to reinstate on a new site.

I also find it handy to be able to work on the layout elsewhere than its normal display position—especially where this is at eye level. Model railroads using 54-inch or greater track heights—as I advocated in the last chapter—are great to look at but a royal pain to work on! Modest-sized demountable sections that can be relocated to a workbench (or failing that, a kitchen table or out in the garage or backyard) are a boon in my book.

The British term for such self-contained movable benchwork is baseboarding, with the individual sections being referred to as, simply, boards; so

when I mention boards in this context, that's what I'm on about!

My preferred method of shelf benchwork construction is a lightweight glued-and-pinned structure based on fabricated plywood L- or T-girders. These form the longitudinal framing, braced with profiled plywood cross-pieces and carrying a plywood or hardboard (Masonite is one brand) fascia. Trackbeds can be the usual plywood/Homasote sandwich, or plain plywood or MDF (medium-density fiberboard) with a resilient underlay system like Woodland Scenics vinyl or Midwest Products excellent cork roadbed. The plywood structure is glued with a high-strength woodworking adhesive (Elmer's yellow carpenter's glue is fine). Light, strong, and free from sag, such a baseboard also can be made to any footprint you like, can accommodate big vertical separations as well as different track levels and just about any kind of scenery.

The relatively deep framing allows plenty of space for wiring runs, switch machines, and built-in sub-base electrical components. With excellent rigidity in the vertical plane, you don't need a lot of support—spans up to eight feet are possible on a girder depth of no more than four inches. However, I don't usually go beyond six feet, which

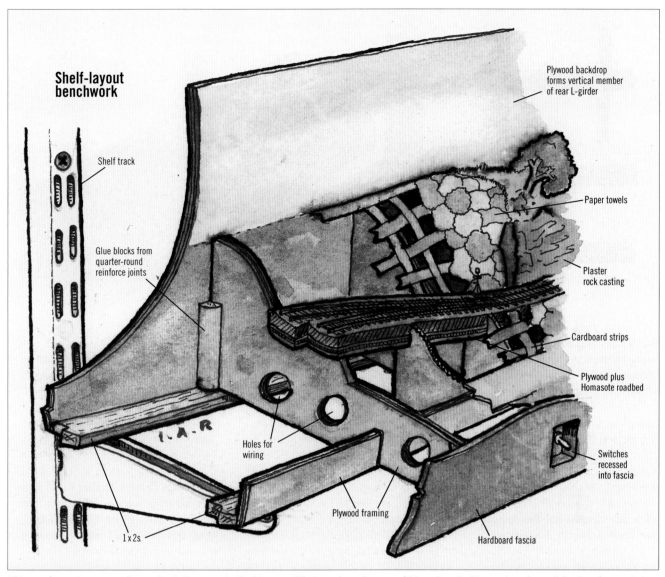

Shelf-layout benchwork

Plywood backdrop forms vertical member of rear L-girder

Shelf track

Paper towels

Plaster rock casting

Glue blocks from quarter-round reinforce joints

Cardboard strips

Plywood plus Homasote roadbed

Holes for wiring

Switches recessed into fascia

Plywood framing

1 x 2s

Hardboard fascia

Hilly or mountainous terrain can be built on a shelf with a modified version of open-grid benchwork. Plywood works well for framing, and the plywood backdrop adds a great deal of structural stability to the assembly. Conventional or foam scenery can be applied over the frame.

I find about as long a board section as can be readily handled. The drawing above shows details of the form of construction.

Section Joints

Of course, if you make your benchwork in handy-sized chunks, you're going to have joints where the trackage will pass from one section to another. Such joints are often cited as a potential source of trouble, but this is pretty much hearsay. In Britain, where sectional portable layouts are the norm and where some very fine wheel and track standards are in use, they've never been seen as a notable problem.

When planning section joints on a shelf layout, it's necessary to first decide

how you're going to support and locate them. There are three basic approaches: You can make each section independent, with at least two supports within its length. You can arrange the joints to coincide with the supporting brackets, so that each bracket supports two sections. Finally, you can piggyback the boards so that a section is supported off of its neighbor. The best approach depends on circumstances.

The first option, independent sections, I've only found necessary for very large and heavy sections—and I try to avoid those anyway. It's also costly in terms of hardware and demanding in terms of accuracy. It's never easy to maintain consistent levels with multiple supports.

The second solution is more economical of hardware and makes for simple alignment and support. This comes at the expense of a little additional carpentry to produce the joiners that sit on top of the brackets and locate the sections.

Piggybacking boards is the most flexible and versatile method of arranging joints, as they can be located independently from the support locations. So long as the foundation board is strong and adequately supported, then the subsidiary boards need only single supporting points, and the joint locations can overhang the foundation board supports by some distance.

Again, a little extra carpentry is needed at the ends of the foundation

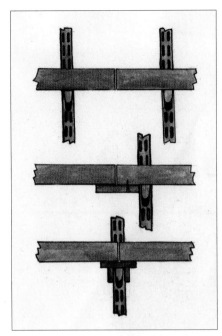

From the top: two independent sections butting together; one section held by the adjoining section; and adjoining ends supported by a common bracket.

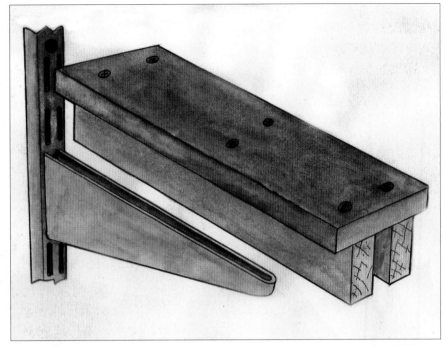

Most commercial track brackets are narrow, and they may be shorter than needed. Adding a simple wood fixture made of plywood or thin dimensional lumber makes it much easier to attach the benchwork assemblies to the bracket.

board to provide the support and location needed for adjoining sections. The main drawback to piggybacked boards is that if you need to move the foundation board, you have to shift all those resting on it too. For this reason, the joint-over-bracket has always been my preferred option for shelf layouts.

Given that most shelf layouts are modest in width and limited in run to their walls and room corners, then it's not difficult to ensure that everything lines up at the joints without the need for sophisticated location devices or ploys like removable track sections to bridge the board-ends. As a breed, shelf layouts don't usually involve large spreads of parallel tracks, so the number involved at any joint is modest.

Accurate tracklaying and firm anchorage of the rail-ends at the joint is the key to trouble-free operation. The baseboards will not normally be free to move out of alignment as they would be on, say, a free-standing portable system. The joint supporting system combined with the reference provided by the wall normally provides all the location needed.

The real essential is to make sure the rail ends on either side of the joint are properly anchored. The usual

method of achieving this is to drive suitable screws or pins firmly into the roadbed—or, better still, right down into the benchwork framing—either directly beneath or close beside the rails and as close to the baseboard end as possible.

The rail ends are then soldered to these fixings, taking great care to get the track alignment spot-on either side of the joint. To ensure this, it's not a bad idea to lay the track clean across the joint, solder it to the anchor points, then separate the sections with a fine cutting disc in a motor tool afterwards. The last touch is to chamfer off the corners of the cut railheads, which helps to ensure a smooth ride over the joint.

However, there are situations where boards are vulnerable to being bumped, are sitting loose on brackets, or are at the end of a run along part of a wall. In these cases, it may be a good idea to provide some means of accurately locating the sections and holding them in alignment. The textbook solution is to use traditional patternmaker's dowels for location and clamping bolts for retention, but pattern dowels aren't so easy to find.

Fortunately, there are several suitable alternatives, of which the simplest

is a good-fitting cupboard door bolt or that old favorite, the split hinge (a butt or flap hinge with a removable pin). The split-hinge system will also hold the boards firmly together. Otherwise, suitable retention can come from nuts and bolts through the end framing, over-center catches front and rear, or our old friend the C-clamp.

In practice, with typical shelf sections with few tracks at joints, I find that aligning things by eye then C-clamping the end frames is as good a solution as any! To facilitate such clamping in over-the-bracket joints, I cut suitable slots in the end frames with a jigsaw, so that I can slip a small clamp through sideways and then bring it across to pull the frames together.

Sectional wiring

Carrying power around to all sections is no big deal either. Usually, the number of circuits that need to go from one section of a shelf layout to another is pretty limited, especially if you're using DCC. In that case, a simple four- or six-core jumper cable will normally handle everything without problem.

If you do need to jump a larger number of discrete circuits—such as when a joint severs multiple track sections or complex signal or switch-control circuits, or where you need to power a range of accessory modules requiring different supply voltages—then ready-wired 20-pin SCART leads and chassis-mount SCART sockets are a good way to go. A SCART gives you 20 ways plus a screen—plenty of capacity for almost any layout. However, SCART leads don't have great current-handling capability, so I wouldn't route a DCC power bus or any other heavy-draw circuit (more than 1 amp) through them.

Rather than getting involved with complex jumping arrangements at joints, I prefer to avoid the need by designing my layout circuitry as a series of self-contained electrical units, one per layout section. Given that shelf layouts are typically of a form that might be described as compact walkaround, then adopting purely local control of turnouts and signaling makes perfect operational sense.

Such localized control can easily be arranged in a way that permits each layout section to be electrically self-contained, with all the relevant switch gear mounted on its fascia. That way, you only need to provide a basic track power bus—plus any separate accessory power needed for switch machines, signals, lighting, or sound modules—to each board. I arrange these feeds as umbilical supplies—cables permanently tethered to the section board at one end, plugging to a central power supply circuit—preferably located on a sub-baseboard service shelf (see page 22)—at the other.

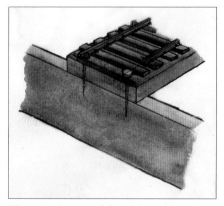

Where tracks cross joints between boards, solder the rail ends to pins that are firmly anchored in the base framing.

Such an arrangement is particularly suited to the concept of taking individual sections to the workbench for construction and maintenance work, as it's easy to arrange to power them up on the bench for checking new wiring or fault-finding.

My own (non-DCC at this juncture) shelf layouts use eight-core umbilical leads and eight-way automotive plug-and-socket joiners (salvaged from auto wrecks in a junk yard). These connectors are robust and trouble-free and incorporate locking devices so they won't come undone. They also have plenty of current-handling capability. At junk yard prices, they're next to being free!

My eight-ways carry four different circuits, including a 16V AC power supply for the vintage plug-in hand-held transistor throttles, the 12V DC-controlled traction power (the output of the throttles, in other words, which feeds a traction bus—either discrete for a single board or common to several boards and to which the individual track blocks are wired).

In addition, the eight-way handles a 24V AC accessory power circuit for solenoid switch machines, uncoupler electromagnets, and the like as well as a 12V DC supply for Tortoise switch machines, signals, lighting, and DC accessory modules. To do all this with DCC you'd only need a power bus and a control bus, as given appropriate interface devices, you could feed any accessories off the power bus.

Linking sections

These are the non-scenic track-only bridging pieces used to join different discrete sections of a non-continuous shelf layout, usually by crossing doors or windows, closets, and access points. Typically, they're removed when the layout is not in use and stored away on service shelves (see section below) or otherwise out of sight.

The usual form of such a linking section is a trough, with a base of half-inch plywood or MDF on which the track and roadbed are laid, sandwiched between sides of thin plywood or Masonite a couple of inches deep, often more. The sides are pinned and

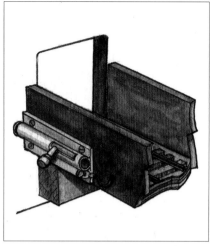

A cabinet slide bolt will align and securely hold lift-out sections in place.

glued to the base, so that they stiffen it as well as providing secure fences on either side to protect equipment from knocks or derailments.

You can make link sections for single or multiple tracks and they can be straight or curved. It's best to make the base wide enough to permit handling of equipment between the sides, but otherwise the dimensions are non-critical. For ease of handling and storage, I find it pays not to make such links too long. Five feet is a good limit to aim for at the design stage, shorter if possible.

I also prefer not to see or hear my trains when they're on such offstage bridging sections, so I make the sides high enough to completely conceal the train and use Peco flextrack in Peco's matching foam roadbed, which gives nearly silent running.

Link sections are usually in bridge form (hence the need for stiffness) and simply rest on ledges or pads at either end fixed to the permanent sections of the layout. Spans of up to five feet are fine with side stiffeners two to three inches deep on the links.

Where longer links are needed (rare, in my experience), then it will be necessary to use deeper sides and often to arrange a suitable mid-point support—such as a shelf bracket or trestle-style leg—to underpin any joint or prevent sagging. To fasten link sections to the fixed portion of the layout, I find simple sliding bolts work well, as shown in the diagram.

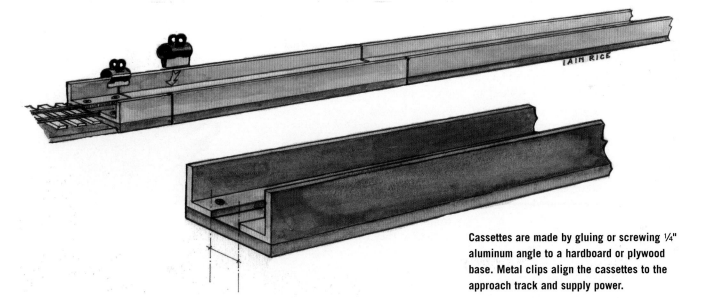

Cassettes are made by gluing or screwing ¼" aluminum angle to a hardboard or plywood base. Metal clips align the cassettes to the approach track and supply power.

Electrically, link sections can be powered through the locating bolts or by a separate plug and jumper lead. Common 3.5mm miniature phono headphone jack plugs work well for this—mono for single track, stereo for double. The plugs go into chassis-mount jack sockets set in the layout framing.

As an added refinement and safety measure, I use the type of socket having an extra pair of circuits that are disconnected when the plug is inserted. These circuits are used to feed a simple 12V DC relay that shuts off the power to the last couple of feet of track on the layout when no link section is plugged in. This avoids the possibility (probability, in my case) of a train being driven off into thin air when the link is not in place.

Fiddle yards and staging

A fundamental rule of layout design goes something like this: "The more compact the layout, the greater the reliance on offstage trackage—fiddle yards or hidden staging—to give good operational potential."

As the vast majority of shelf-based model railroads come into the compact category—with quite a few being sub-compact or even minimal—then accommodating such offstage trackage is usually a key design requirement.

I am often asked at layout design clinics about the difference between staging and fiddling. Staging merely provides a temporary off-scene parking place for trains, where they can be held unchanged until required to re-appear by the timetable or operating sequence. A fiddle yard, by contrast, is a destination, where trains will be broken up and re-marshaled into completely different formations. The purpose of a fiddle yard is to represent—functionally—all that part of the railroad that can't be included in the modeled scenes.

Practically, the vital difference is that staging tracks need only occasional access for maintenance or in case of a mishap, whereas a fiddle yard must be easy to get at and have facilities for stabling, uncoupling, swapping, and storing equipment. Operationally, you can use a fiddle yard for staging, but mostly you can't use a staging track for fiddling.

The size and type of fiddle yard or staging needed for a layout will be dictated by the nature of the layout and the style of operation. An end-to-end or continuous-run layout might well get away without any such off-scene trackage, although in most cases at least a little will add considerably to the operational potential. At the other extreme, a stub-end layout—like my own Roque Bluffs branchline terminal—will depend entirely on a fiddle yard to provide any operational scope other than as a pure switching puzzle. Many of the layout themes that lend themselves particularly well to shelf format call for offstage facilities of some sort, as can be seen from the portfolio of plans at the rear of this book.

Fortunately, the shelf format lends itself to the provision of compact fiddle yards or staging. In particular, track-mounted shelving offers many possibilities for vertical solutions such as train-stackers or cassettes, both of which provide ample capacity in a small footprint, a footprint, moreover, that is long and narrow and thus ideally suited to typical shelf proportions.

Where space is not at a premium, you can use ordinary turnouts to lay out single-ended or ladder-style offstage yards. But where these are intended for fiddling rather than staging, don't forget that the parallel tracks will need to be sufficiently well spread to permit access for equipment handling—4" center-to-center in HO and not a lot less in N. The trains may get smaller, but human fingers stay the same size!

The advantage of the turnout-based yard is that it calls for less hands-on manipulation to align tracks and—using switch machines and a suitable remote control set-up—trains can be routed in and out of the yard from a distant operating position. But that facility comes at a high cost in terms of reduced yard capacity on a given footprint.

Cassette-and-shelf fiddle yards

A more usual solution for shelf-based fiddle yards is some sort of movable

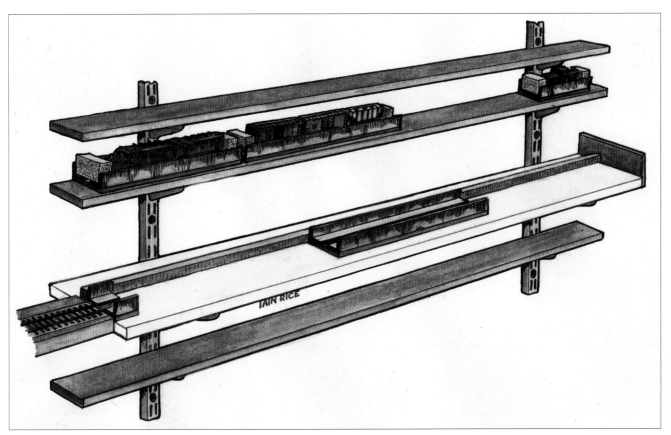

Cassettes can be different lengths to hold locomotives, engine consists, or entire trains. Shelves above and below track level hold the cassettes until they're needed.

storage system, of which the train cassette is the best-established and most versatile. This useful device, first outlined by British modeler Chris Pendlenton some 20 years ago, is really a miniaturized version of the link section already described, using inch-and-a-half aluminum angle to form both the rails and the side fences/stiffeners of the individual units. (That's for HO and O scales; you can user a smaller section angle for N).

The angle is fixed—glued or screwed—to a sub-base of suitable insulating material, such as hardboard, MDF, or plywood, with the inner edges of the angle set apart by the appropriate track gauge. Around 48 inches is the practical cassette-length limit for me—it depends how long your arms are when it comes to picking the thing up! Four feet will accommodate a locomotive, four to five freight cars, and a caboose in HO, so to handle longer trains, several shorter cassettes may be located end-to-end.

Anyway, it's a good idea to have small, dedicated cassettes to hold engines, cabooses, and other pieces of equipment that need frequent handling during fiddle yard operation. The different cassette lengths are usually described by their function. Whole-train is a single long cassette for the train together with locomotives and cabooses. Consist-only is a cassette long enough for the revenue consist but relying on separate units to hold motive power and tail-end equipment. Part-train or cut cassettes are enough to hold cuts of cars forming sections of a longer train. Individual cassettes handle motive power (single engines or multiple-unit lashups) and cabooses. The whole idea is that you manipulate the cassettes with the equipment in them rather than handling the models directly.

These movable cassettes sit on a simple flat deck—one aspect of shelf railroading for which plastic-sheathed particle board is ideal. At the end of the deck adjoining the layout is a short length of fixed cassette as a lead-in track—often referred to as a dock, which is carefully married to the entry track from the layout proper. Along the rear of the deck is an alignment fence, a length of stripwood positioned so that when cassettes are pushed up against it they are correctly positioned in relation to each other and to the fixed lead-in.

Spring-metal document clips can be used between cassettes to hold everything in line and to transmit power from the lead-in, which carries the feed from the traction or DCC power bus. On non-DCC layouts like mine, the feed to this lead-in is wired as a separate track block, so that turning this block off effectively isolates the whole fiddle yard.

In use, a suitable string of cassettes is assembled to accommodate an incoming train, run into them using the normal layout control system. The train can then be uncoupled to break it down into the required units for re-marshalling or stowage. This is a job for which a magnetic or mechanical uncoupling pick is ideal, or you can simply lift car ends to disengage the coupler knuckles.

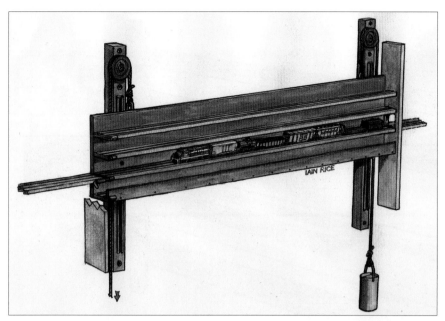

The "train stacker" holds multiple trains in staging in a tight space. The stacker slides up and down on a common ball-bearing drawer track, with sliding bolts to hold it in alignment.

long. In the context of my Roque Bluffs, where a seven-car train with a caboose fills a siding, it means that a typical string will be limited to four cassettes: a locomotive, two part-train, and the caboose or about 53 inches long in all. The fiddle deck in this case is a tight 56 inches, which only leaves room for a short lead-in track.

Train stackers

Shelf-based cassette fiddle yards typically call for the fiddling deck at layout level and several shelves above or below to provide storage for additional cassettes. Much the same vertical space can accommodate another approach to housing and handling offstage trains on a long-but-narrow footprint—the train stacker.

This is similar in form to an old-fashioned sash window, consisting of a backing board carrying a number of train-bearing shelves, the whole thing being suspended on ropes passing over pulleys and connected to counterweights. The stacker slides up and

With the train broken down into cuts of cars or individual items of equipment in the various cassettes, the spring clips are removed and the cassettes separated. For straightforward re-marshalling, the cassettes can be simply slid around on the deck into the required order, the clips reconnected, and the segments of the train coupled together. To change things out—substituting different equipment for all or part of the consist—then some or all of the cassettes can be lifted off the deck onto storage shelves above or below layout level, and other cassettes holding different equipment substituted.

To prevent cars running off the end of the cassettes while they're being moved, end stops are used—simply blocks of firm foam rubber cut to be a nice tight fit between the side fences of the cassette, pushed up tight against the car ends, and held in place by friction. Cheap pan scourers are a good source of suitable blocks of foam.

The ideal is to have sufficient cassettes and on-shelf storage capacity to house all your equipment, so that no matter how intensively the layout is used, the models themselves never need to be handled. I know of a few modelers who take this concept to the ultimate by providing a dedicated cassette for each individual item of equipment; however, this requires more dedication

than I'm inclined to! It also makes for a lot of high-precision work in the fiddle yard. I prefer to keep my equipment in short cuts of two, three, or four cars in part-train cassettes 15 to 25 inches

A narrow storage shelf under the layout keeps power supplies, tools, and other materials handy but out of normal view. It's easy to add to the existing shelf tracks.

down in a frame that locates it—ball-bearing drawer or sliding door track works well for this—and that carries the pulleys for the counterweights. The lead-in track is also attached to this frame, and the tracks are held in alignment by a simple sliding bolt. The counterweights are slightly heavier than the fully loaded stacker, so it tends to stay in the up position and is pulled downward to align the upper tracks with the lead-in.

Stackers can be configured for staging or fiddling use, the difference lying in the spacing of the shelves, their width, and the number of tracks on them. Staging stackers, where no access is needed for fiddling trains, can have shelves on centers with as little as three inches of vertical clearance in HO. At the same scale, a six-inch wide stacker shelf could carry up to four parallel tracks. Six such shelves would require a vertical distance of just 18 inches. To allow all the tracks to align with the lead-in, you need that amount of clearance above the fixed track level, but only 15 inches below it.

Stackers eight or more feet in length are quite possible, and with a 96-inch long footprint just over six inches wide, you could accommodate no less than 192 feet of staging trackage—enough to hold about 300 mixed 40- and 50-foot HO freight cars. A stacker of the same size in N scale, with correspondingly tighter centers, could have a capacity of well over a thousand cars! (Micro-Trains car collectors please note.) But such monster stackers would be heavy, calling for serious counterweights and massive support framing braced to a strong floor. The far more modest affair suited to a compact shelf layout is light and compact enough to hang on the wall or to sit on shelf brackets. Ten six-foot tracks on five twin-track decks would still give you a capacity of more than 100 cars in HO—enough for most of us!

Fiddle stackers, with their need to allow good access for car manipulation, don't permit such tight clearances vertically or horizontally. It's best to stick with one track per shelf and shelf spacing of four inches or more for HO, only marginally less for N. With such a

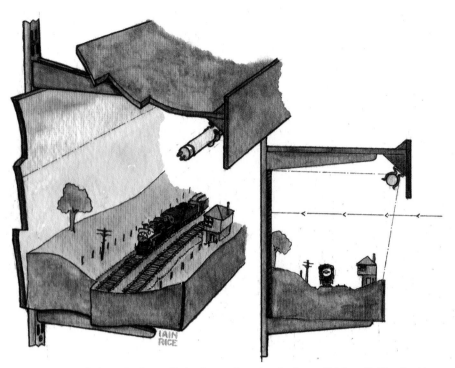

A top-deck shelf above the layout limits dust and carries the layout lighting. Making it wider than the bottom shelf ensures that the front edge of the layout is adequately illuminated.

low density of trackage, fiddle stackers don't have nearly as much capacity as staging.

However, it's quite possible to combine the stacker concept with cassettes, by placing cassettes rather than fixed trackwork on the stacker shelves. This gives the best of both worlds: the quick change facility of the stacker, which enables a pre-marshaled train to be quickly aligned with the exit and dispatched onto the layout, with the manipulation and stock-storage capabilities of the cassette system.

Service and storage shelves

A useful adjunct to any layout is additional shelving to provide a home for extra equipment, layout ancillaries, and necessities like uncoupling picks, wheel- and track-cleaning devices, and tools. With strip-shelf as layout support, providing this facility amounts to no more than buying a few extra brackets and additional shelving for which plastic-faced particle board is just fine.

I recommend a service shelf, a narrow (typically six-inch wide) shelf mounted close under the layout along its whole length. It performs much the same function as under-street ducting does in a city, an out-of-sight but accessible place to locate cabling and to place power supply units and other electrical devices.

My various layout bus circuits run along the service shelf, with outlets at convenient locations to receive the umbilical leads from each individual baseboard. The shelf also carries a multi-outlet mains power strip (or several such strips in daisy-chain formation) into which are plugged all the transformer units providing the various outputs needed for the layout functions as well as the feeds to the overhead layout lighting. The lead from this power strip forms the only connection between the model railroad and the house wiring. Pull that one plug, and the whole layout is electrically dead.

Storage shelves dedicated to model railroad use are darned useful, and I find the combination of cassettes holding the actual equipment sitting on dedicated shelves adjacent to the fiddleyard to be a great way to keep my models free from dust or harm. I keep the spacing of these cassette storage shelves as tight as practicable—typically about two slots on the track between brackets, which gives five-inch centers, enough room for handling, but not enough to let anyone put anything else

Presentation is important with shelf layouts. This is the author's "Trerice" layout with the top deck matching the contoured layout fascia. It's finished in a neutral color and set off by contrasting drapes. The track level height is 54" above the floor.

on top of your models! I use nine-inch wide shelves to hold individual-item cassettes, which in my case are typically six inches for a caboose and nine inches for a diesel or small steam locomotive stored end-on. All longer cassettes stow lengthwise on the shelves, and I restrict myself to two cassettes side-by-side on a six-inch shelf.

Keeping the shelf spacing tight also helps keep the dust at bay. Such storage shelves can hide beneath the layout—preferably behind the drapes where these are provided (see section below). Adjacent to the fiddle yard, I have a couple of exposed cassette storage shelves, so I took the trouble to use good veneered boards so that the finished shelves have a neat and pleasing appearance.

Presentation

Shelf-based layouts are often seen as a good solution where a model railroad has to be housed in the living quarters of a home, sharing space with domestic activities rather than tucked away in a basement, loft, or garage. This means that the layout has to fit with the room's décor.

Roque Bluffs, my own HO shelf layout, formerly shared wall space with the library in my study/home office, and thus called for careful integration into the bookshelf system. The layout fascia and the overhead dust protection and lighting shelf were finished to blend with the room colors, and all the wiring, ancillaries, and storage were carefully concealed or neatly finished.

Good presentation is an asset for any model railroad, but for one on display in the home, it's an absolute essential. Fortunately, wall-mounted shelf systems once again makes our life easier. For a start, there's no forest of legs and L-girders that has to be concealed, and much of the shelving and support hardware we're using is already designed and finished to a domestic standard.

The typical footprint and modest cross-section of a typical shelf layout also don't intrude greatly into a room, while the simple-to-achieve combination of a good backdrop with well-proportioned and neatly-finished top and bottom fascias should ensure that what is seen will be good to look at. Where appropriate, a below-layout drape or cabinets conceals storage. Never forget that the provision of such storage may well help swing things when right-of-way negotiations are in progress!

Fascias

I never regard fascias—either the contoured layout fascia following the outline of the landscaping or the straight-edged lighting valance above it—as optional. To me, they are a fundamental part of the layout, requiring careful planning and neat execution.

Planning? Well, for a start, they need to be dimensioned to a good proportion. On a shelf layout with the suggested 10- to 12-inch gap between valance and fascia, the layout fascia should have at least a four-inch average depth, and the upper lighting valance will probably need an inch or so more. Remember, it has to not only conceal the lighting but also cut off the sight lines to avoid a visible top of sky.

If you don't want your foreground in shadow, the valance also needs to be set two to three inches in front of the layout fascia—see lighting section that follows. All of these considerations need to be taken into account when designing the upper shelf.

Fascias also need to be fixed neatly with concealed fastenings such as lost-head pins—something that needs consideration when the benchwork is being planned and built to ensure you have something to fix to.

In the context of a shelf layout using the sort of local control I've described, the layout fascia is also the place to mount switch gear, manual turnout controls, receptacles for throttles, and so on. To keep things neat and to protect the switch gear from accidental damage, I like to recess all these fittings into the fascia in small, neat panels.

I've already likened layout fascias to picture frames—and just like a good picture frame, a layout fascia needs to set off and complement a model, not compete with it.

There's a long tradition of veneered or plywood layout fascias polished or varnished to a high finish—which I find overpowering. Wood-grain often has pronounced textures that can exhibit strong distracting coloring.

My preference is for a fascia with smooth finish—hardboard or thin MDF sheet—finished with an even, flat coat of a neutral-color paint. I try to choose something sympathetic to the color values in the model itself. Earth shades, most grays, air force blue, sage, or pine green and even a gentle turquoise can all work well. You'll notice these are all colors typically used in military camouflage schemes. In other words, they're shades that blend in rather than stand out.

The paint I use is one of the new-generation one-coat satin-finish vinyls made for interior woodwork. Although they can cover in one hit, I find a second coat worth the effort. A final coat of a hard-wearing matte or semi-gloss varnish is also worthwhile to protect the fascia finish from handling wear and snagging damage. I use acrylic polyurethane floor varnish for this.

Backdrop

I also regard a backdrop as an absolute essential for a shelf layout. The question is, what's the best way of arranging it? With a wall-mounted shelf layout, you have two options: fix your backdrop to the layout itself, or hang it off the wall. Both approaches have their advantages, but for me, the wall wins because of my preference for building the layout in movable segments.

Fixing a backdrop to these would mean you have a sectional backdrop, and a sectional backdrop is one that has joints. Getting rid of these joints is not so easy—although more possible on a shelf layout, where the backdrop is relatively shallow and the top of the scene is defined by an upper fascia. In

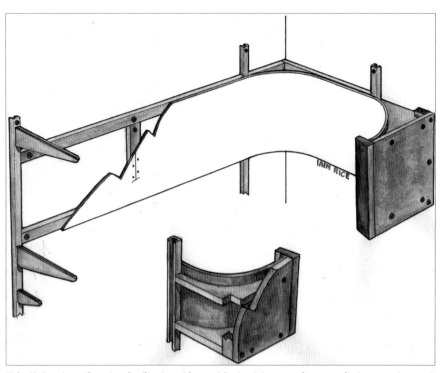

Thin (2-3mm) medium-density fiberboard is good for backdrops, as it can easily be curved around corners. A 1 x 2 frame attached to the wall holds the backdrop, with brackets in the corners.

these circumstances, modeled elements of the scene—a tall building, factory smokestack, lofty tree, or steep rocky outcrop—can be arranged to take up most if not all of the visible height without appearing odd. Placing such a feature in front of a backdrop joint can thus hide the irksome fissure.

How workable this sort of solution is depends on the nature of the model railroad. It's no problem if you're modeling a downtown industrial zone, mountainous scene, or a logging line in tall timber. However, it's more of a problem if you're trying to represent open country—particularly somewhere flat, like the Maine coast, the Southwest desert, or most of the Midwest.

Even after years of trying, I haven't figured a good way of hiding those inevitable cracks in the sky on an open-landscape backdrop. So I avoid the problem by using a continuous backdrop supported off the wall and thus entirely independent of the layout sections. The drawings show how I arrange this type of backdrop, which is framed out in small-section lumber (I use three-quarter by inch-and-a-half material, which matches the depth of the shelf track). The framing is surfaced with a smooth-faced, flex-

ible sheet that can readily be curved to make coved corners. Masonite is OK for straight backdrops and wide corners, but the best material I've found so far is thin MDF sheet.

A grade around 2mm thick used as a backing board by picture framers is just right. It comes in 4 x 8 sheets, and any good lumberyard should be able to source it for you. You can cut it easily with a heavy utility knife, which avoids the dust hazard associated with machining MDF. This 2mm board is so flexible you can form it around curves as tight as a three-inch radius, and it's easy to fix in place with lost-head (also called panel or veneer) pins.

For tight corners (common on shelf layouts), I frame the coving with profile pieces cut from half-inch plywood, as in the sketch. Using eight-foot strips, joints will be rare, but where unavoidable, they can be made on a splice plate and carefully filled with spackling or fine-surface filler and sanded smooth.

You can seal hardboard or MDF with normal household latex paint applied with a roller, which gives a smooth overall texture and avoids brush marks. I usually prime with a couple of coats of brilliant white to give the truest base for the backdrop art, then use

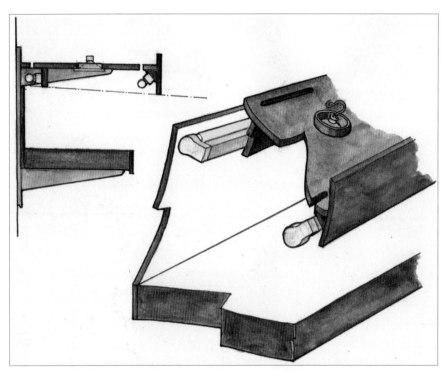

Fluorescent tube fixtures placed behind the valance will illuminate the scene evenly and without harsh shadows. Deep scenes may require a second set of light tubes at the rear.

a mix of household latex and artist's acrylic paints (usually, you can mix the two) to create a sky, using the roller to spread and blend the colors.

This is not the place for an essay on backdrop painting, but for what it's worth, here are the key things I've found essential to success. Keep it simple: Use restrained colors to ensure distance recession. Also, choose colors that are matched and blended with those included in the modeled scene. Avoid brush strokes and other textures like the plague. Steer clear of buildings or other elements calling for perspective drawing, which can only ever look right from a single viewpoint and extremely odd from anyplace else!

Lighting

Lighting may have been left until last, but that by no means makes it least in importance! Good lighting can bring a layout to life, give it sparkle and impact, convincing colors and an authentic atmosphere. Bad lighting can glare, make colors look odd, cast unwanted shadows, and give off too much heat.

This last point is a particularly important one for a shelf railroad with a top deck set-up as advocated in this

book, as the lighting will be mounted close to the model—typically no more than about 12 inches away.

Some popular layout-lighting sources—particularly high-wattage household-type tungsten lamps and low-voltage or mains-powered quartz-halogen fittings—kick out high enough levels of radiated heat to cause serious snags at this sort of distance. We're talking problems of the track buckling, plastic freight car drooping, scenery wilting, or wood-structure-curling-up kind. Not the sort of things you can ignore!

Fortunately, close-set lighting has advantages as well as drawbacks. Physics says that the amount of light falling on a surface decreases by the square of the distance from the light source. So, if you move your lights twice as far away, you'll need four times the amount of light output to get the same level of illumination. Standing this equation on it's head, if you halve the distance between model and source, you only need a quarter as much light.

As light output is directly related to lamp power, this means that in the sort of situation on our typical shelf layout, we need only a relatively low-powered lighting set up. Since the thermal output from light fittings is

also related to their power, then this helps moderate the unwanted heat problem. Choosing cooler-running light sources and arranging suitable ventilation can help eliminate unwanted heat altogether.

Light sources and positioning

Different types of light source give different qualities of light, so choosing the right one relates not only to the lamp positioning, but also to the desired effect, which, in turn, comes back to layout subject. A lighting set-up that does a good job of creating a July high noon in the Nevada desert is hardly going to be convincing for a mild mountain spring day in Washington state or a bit of New England November gloom.

Leaving aside the raw solar glare of southern summer skies, mostly we need somewhat cooler light sources, more biased to the blue rather than the yellow end of the color spectrum. Such cooler tones are associated more with sources like daylight balance strip lights or energy-saving fluorescent bulbs and also with those new kids on the block, high-intensity LEDs.

All these are good choices for shelf layout lighting as they run as cool as they look and pose no problems when mounted at short range. Also, they are diffuse sources rather than the focused beams associated with quartz-halogen or tungsten spotlight fittings. That is, they radiate equally in all directions and don't throw stark, intense shadows.

For a shelf layout, with its characteristic long-but-narrow scene, a series of small-diameter strip lights mounted just behind the lighting fascia forms pretty much an ideal form of general illumination. I use 13-watt, 21-inch long T4 tri-phosphor tubes only a half-inch in diameter mounted in slim under-cabinet fittings. With the lighting fascia overhanging the layout fascia by three inches or so as already suggested, you get good illumination of objects at the front of the scene, whereas locating light sources directly over the center of the layout often leaves such foreground features in shadow.

Mounting the lights above the front edge of the scene directly behind the top fascia also makes it easy to conceal the actual fittings and keeps the light sources out of the line of vision. Bright lights in the field of view are very distracting. The T4 tubes have a 5400K rating (very close to a daylight source) and produce very little heat, easily dissipated by modest ventilation slots shown in the sketch.

Front-mounted T4 strip lights alone will do a good enough job of illuminating the whole scene width as well as the backdrop on layouts up to around 18 inches deep. Painting the unseen underside of the top deck gloss white helps by reflecting maximum light onto the layout. Deeper scenes will usually call for a second row of strip lights at the rear of the scene, concealed by a baffle strip along the underside of the top deck, as in the diagram.

Positioning these rear lights as close as practicable to the top of the backdrop provides a light wash down the latter that can be effective at killing unwanted cast shadows. Indeed, even quite narrow scenes can benefit from rear illumination where backdrop shadows are a problem (but see other shadow-catching dodges in Chapter 3).

For added punch to represent sunlight, low-voltage tungsten-halogen wide-angle diffuse down lights can be mounted into the top deck shelf at centers according roughly to the scene width. The low-profile or recessed fittings for use beneath kitchen cabinets work well. You don't need high-power bulbs—the basic G9 25W bulb is fine and doesn't kick out too much heat.

Shelf-lighting hardware

In terms of actual hardware, I've had good results with the miniature strip light systems designed to fit beneath kitchen cabinets. They come in convenient plug-together form; the one I often use comes from Ikea.

These fittings are also light in weight and run cool, while their output of around 12W per tube is plenty when they're mounted close. They provide a good level of overall northern daylight illumination and—being continuous rather than point sources—don't throw conflicting shadows. (Some layouts I've seen are apparently located on a planet illuminated by more than one sun!)

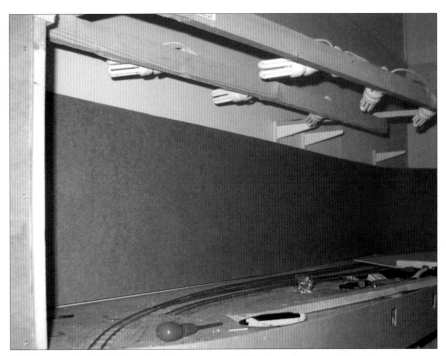

Here's an overhead lighting raft using fluorescent bulbs for a deep-scene shelf layout, supported by shelf tracks. The backdrop is 2mm medium-density fiberboard.

Where strip lights fall down somewhat is in illuminating scenes representing sunnier climes where stark cast shadows and a lot more sparkle are needed to get the right effect. Here, you need something with more punch. It may be necessary to mix two or more types of light source to provide the right effect.

When it comes to punch, there's nothing better than quartz- or tungsten-halogen. Using the strip lights for overall illumination but brightening up the levels with occasional quartz or tungsten fittings at suitable intervals works well without resulting in the sort of troublesome heat levels that an all-halogen set-up produces.

The thing to avoid is the use of focused-beam spotlight fittings or self-contained halogen spot lamps, which can produce devastatingly high localized heat levels. What we want are wide-angle surface-mounted halogen down lights.

Again, these are sold as low-profile fittings designed to mount beneath kitchen cabinets, with side-mounted halogen bulbs and a faceted reflector giving a more diffuse beam. Such units using 20 or 25W lamps mounted every couple of feet or so along the layout, usually give quite enough added sparkle, and keep the heat problem at bay.

Just to be on the safe side, if I'm using these fixtures, I move the top deck up a couple more inches and deepen the upper fascia accordingly, to get the lamps a further from the layout. The radiated heat also diminishes with the square of the distance.

The new generation of high intensity LEDs also offers potential for shelf layout lighting, being compact, cool-running, non-directional sources that can be found in a rapidly growing range of colors. They weigh next to nothing, use a miniscule amount of power, and run cold, so you can mix and group them as needed for the effect you're after.

I'm still experimenting with these, but I see them as the way to go for the extended and re-situated Roque Bluffs. The trick seems to be hitting on the right combination of colors and spacing to get sufficient illumination but an appropriate color balance.

The domestic fittings offered so far all seem to be very blue, OK for northern Maine; not so good for Nevada! But with the rate of development and the heavy reliance being placed on LEDs for energy-efficient lighting, it won't be long before there are LED sources with warmer color balances.

CHAPTER THREE

Planning a shelf layout

Flat prairie railroading, featuring a relatively narrow right-of-way and straight track, is easy to model on a shelf railway. This is the Burlington Northern Santa Fe in central Minnesota. *Jeff Wilson*

Planning a shelf layout is much the same job as planning any other kind of model railroad, except a whole raft of restrictions, solutions, dodges, and approaches apply specifically to the shelf format. Those are the things I want to look at in more detail in this chapter. First, however, a word or two on the generalities of layout design—beginning with the prototype.

This Midwestern small-town scene, with its classic depot and wood grain elevators, can be captured on a shelf railroad. This is Baltic, S.D., on the Milwaukee Road in 1943. *Henry J. McCord*

Yards are modelable on shelf layouts, but they should be small, straight, and narrow. This is the New York, Ontario & Western Maybrook (N.Y.) yard in 1957. *Jim Shaughnessy*

My own goals in layout design have always put realism and atmosphere alongside interesting operation at the top of the want list. And I've always found that marrying an appropriate subject with the space I have is the key to achieving that goal.

Picking the right "what" to model is a vital first step in achieving a happy marriage. In this context, I'm not defining the "what" so much in terms of prototype road name or era so much as the nature of the railroad subject you're trying to replicate.

For instance, modeling the Southern Pacific could mean anything from Cab-Forwards thundering over Donner Pass to modern six-axle units hauling lumber products out of Siskiyou country to vintage EMD switchers working street trackage on the Bay Area belt line. These could all be represented in shelf format, but not on the same size and shape of shelf!

To model Donner, shelf or no shelf, you'll still need a basement-sized site, but a little bit of the Bay Belt could pretty much go on the mantelpiece. The key to success would be to find an aspect of the SP that you like and that can be reasonably represented in the space you have. Trying to cram an unsuitable subject on a wrong-sized site is a recipe for frustration. Finding the right "what" can be tricky. One often has to look well past the obvious to find something suitable.

Mocking up a scene at full size with flextrack and crude structures is good way to check curves and clearances and will give you a good idea of how the finished scene will appear.

Site size and shape are always critical givens in layout design, but shelf sites are generally more constricted than most. As I've already suggested, you're never going to place some aspects of the prototype on a shelf. Which begs the question: What elements or styles of prototype railroading do happily fit the classic shelf footprint? Here are some more possibilities:

- typical lineside depots, lineside industries and industrial interchanges generally
- passing sidings
- smaller classification yards—six or eight tracks
- compact downtown terminal or through stations
- branchline terminals
- non-roundhouse engine terminals and shop complexes
- all manner of docks, harbors and waterfronts
- as general railroad subjects, some main lines, most secondary and branch lines

Multi-deck shelf-mounted trackage can increase route mileage on operation-oriented layouts. Tony Koester's new HO Nickel Plate Road layout uses shelves this way, although the large main yard is on conventional benchwork. *Tony Koester*

- short lines
- mining, industrial, and logging lines of all sorts, including coal-country branches, mine loading facilities, and minor classification yards
- tight urban switching complexes
- interurbans, streetcars and similar electric railroads
- narrow-gauge railroads of most kinds
- historic railroads of the pre-1900 era
- portage and pioneer railroads

Shelf layouts do have a couple of incidental layout-planning virtues as a consequence of their restricted footprints. The first of these is that they almost-invariably keep you "sincere." That's the term layout-design guru John Armstrong used to describe model railroads where trains run through every scene or location only once, rather than taking several curtain calls in different parts of the ballpark.

Sincere main lines are widely held to be a prerequisite of realistic design and authentic operation. Shelves pretty much guarantee that this will be the case—there just ain't room to be insincere!

By the same token, you're led away from that other prevalent layout-design trap, which I call "over-egging the pudding." This is the temptation to keep adding things—spurs, loops, structures, special facilities of all kinds—simply because the space is there and it seems a shame to waste it.

Real railroads always aim to operate with the minimum of trackage and facilities that will enable them to do the job at hand, so if you're trying to plan a realistic model railroad, you need to do likewise. Shelf sites remove the temptation to do otherwise.

Whole layout design

In my book, setting, presentation, background, display height, lighting, scenic features, structures, and a convincing geographic and historical rationale are all fundamentals in the design process, just as important as the business of merely arranging the rails.

Sure, the track plan is a key element, but a mere track plan is a long way from being a full-fledged layout design. While track planning, you need to keep all the other criteria in mind, so that what emerges is a fully rounded 3-D picture.

To help this process, I use a number of techniques aside from basic track plans at the drawing-board or computer. These include perspective sketching, the construction of simple small-scale planning models, and—easiest of all—mocking up ideas at full size using flextrack, crude card structures, and scenery sketched-in from scrunched-up newspaper as shown in the picture on the previous page.

This works particularly well when trying to envision railroads on shelves, as you can simply set a suitably-sized plain plank in place at the proper height on the shelf brackets to provide a very clear idea of what your finished proposal will look like and how it will function.

Mocking up at full-size allows you to check train lengths and clearance points, arrive at a pleasing visual composition, and position functional features, viewblocks, and structures. A mock-up can also help determine what needs to go where on the all-important backdrop.

Of course, this being the 21st century, you can do all this in virtual reality mode on your computer screen using suitable layout planning software.

I just find this electronic approach less immediate (and usually much slower) than playing around with chopped-up cereal cartons, parcel tape, and newspaper.

Shelf layout design criteria

Whenever space is restricted—as it almost inevitably is on a shelf rail-road—then you need to design tight. With a traditional room-size or larger layout, you're essentially creating a tract of landscape with a railroad running through it. There's room for the railroad to breathe, and you don't normally have to plan everything to the nearest inch. Whole areas of the layout are given over to the scenic setting, allowing you to model, say, a complete township, a large industry complex or just a few hundred acres of rolling countryside.

On a shelf, however, you do need to be precise in planning. You also need to focus on essentials as usually there just isn't room for many extraneous bits and pieces. In terms of what you can model, shelf railroading is essentially stripped-down to the right-of-way, immediately adjacent structures or features, boundary fences, and a few inches of fore and background scenery.

This tight focus is not the drawback it might sound, as such a style of layout—especially at eye-level—keeps you close to the action and gives you that real trackside experience.

Modeling large areas of scenery is not every modeler's cup of tea anyway—there are quite a few model railroaders of my acquaintance (mostly keen operators) who've chosen the shelf format precisely because it is both sincere and railroad-centered. It doesn't require them to spend a lot of time building large tracts of scenery when that's not their interest.

Bill Darnaby's Maumee Route and Tony Koester's Nickel Plate Road both tread that route, while even more famously John Armstrong's iconic O scale Canadaigua Southern was to all intents and purposes a shelf layout; a pretty convoluted sort of a shelf, admittedly, but nowhere on the CS did the scenery amount to much more than a shallow strip either side of the (utterly

Gently curving track that doesn't parallel the shelf edge, subtle changes in scenery levels, and broken scenic outlines all help lose the "shelf look." This scenic mastery in N scale is on Lance Mindheim's Monon layout. *Lance Mindheim*

sincere) right-of-way. That's not to say that shelf railroads can't have a scenic bias. They can, as a glance at Lance Mindheim's wonderful N scale Monon layout will soon testify. It's just that you have to strike a delicate balance between trackage and scenery and make full use of space-saving scenic aids like backdrops and low-relief modeling. More on scenic space in a moment.

Track planning for shelf sites

Track planning for tight sites like shelves also requires a bit of extra care in making the right trade-offs between factors like curve radii, turnout numbers, loop and siding lengths, and fiddle yard capacities.

Curves negotiating corners of 90 degrees or more take up a lot of space—and the amount of real-estate needed for a given radius doesn't change whether the curve is part of a small layout or a large one. Using wide-radius curves is always nice—in the case of some types of equipment, it's essential—but in the context of a compact shelf layout, wide curves can be problematic.

I've already mentioned the room-corner situation, where easy curves

often call for extra-wide shelves or angled span boards rather than simple butt joints. The other snag with wide curves on a modest pike is the amount of tangent (straight alignment) you're left with between them—the length you need to accommodate yards, depots, and passing sidings. Choosing the proper curves for corners thus needs to strike a fine balance between good appearance and proper functioning of equipment while leaving enough room for whatever it is you need to fit in between them.

Unless you're living in some zap-pow piece of modern architecture, an adobe hacienda, or a cave, chances are your walls will be more-or-less straight and your shelves likewise. Running tangent trackage parallel to such a straight wall seems an obvious track-planning ploy, but it's something I try to avoid. Too many parallels tend to emphasise the squared-off shape and proportions of the typical shelf site, something I'd rather disguise.

I've already suggested that creating benchwork with a gently-curving front edge to help lose the rectangular-strip footprint and laying tracks either at an angle to the wall—or, better still, as gentle sweeping curves that wind their

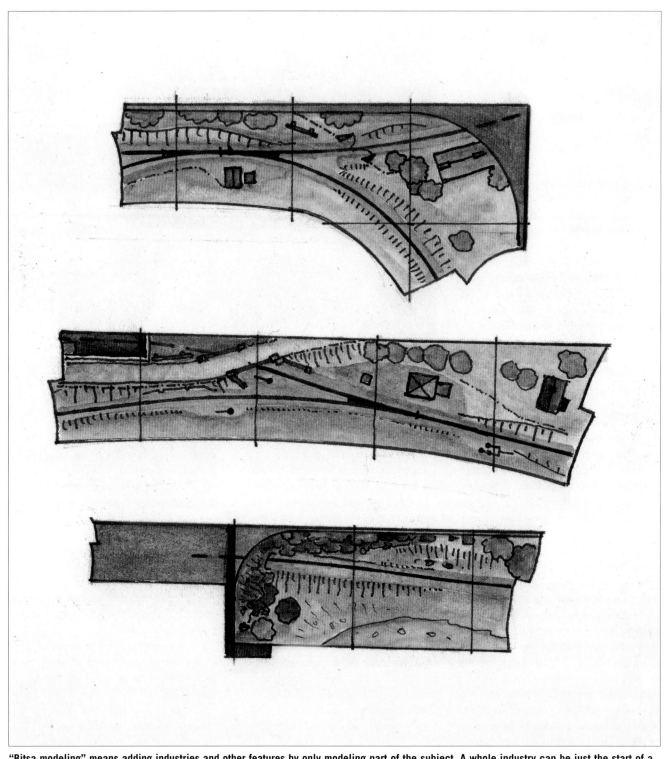

"Bitsa modeling" means adding industries and other features by only modeling part of the subject. A whole industry can be just the start of a spur (top), a branch line can be a turnout and a tower (middle), and a mountain division some rockwork over a tunnel mouth (bottom).

way along the shelf—will help get away from the strip-terrain feel.

By and large, I find I can live without much in the way of dead-straight trackage anyway, although I grant you there are some subjects (mostly Midwestern or modern) for which it's needed for prototype realism. These

straight tracks don't have to parallel that wall, though.

The other track-planning essential for compact layouts is achieving proper balance between the various elements of the design, on-scene and off. There's not a whole lot of point in squeezing the scenic part of the layout to make

room for a passing siding or runaround track capable of handling 10-car trains if the fiddle yard will only hold eight. Similarly, a spur that will just nicely hold four cars is no more use if it's a bit longer but still won't quite hold five. Those extra few inches might well be put to better use—permitting a gentler

Make sure objects, such as the tree or center utility pole, don't cast shadows on the backdrop. You can place an object directly against the backdrop to avoid having a shadow, like the pole at left, or add a 3-D fixture like the billboard at right to catch the shadow.

turnout angle, perhaps? It's surprising how often just carefully optimizing spur lengths and turnout numbers can make room for an extra feature, such as another industry, an engine servicing track, or an operating feature like a track scale. The odd egg won't hurt the pudding!

A layout-planning trick that can work well in a compact shelf layout context is to use the "bitsa" approach. Rather than trying to include the whole of something—a subsidiary route, lineside industry, scenic feature, structure, or railroad facility—you only include enough modeled elements to suggest what it is you're representing while leaving most of it unmodeled.

A lineside industry generating traffic (and hence operating potential) could be represented on the model simply by a turnout and the start of a spur—decorated with a suitable sign claiming the track for Gargantua Industries Inc. The spur track simply runs off scene (see the section on exits below), maybe ending as hidden trackage within the modeled scene or, better still, sneaking off into the fiddle yard.

Even if the hidden track will only conceal a couple of cars, that's still a switching move. Similarly, a subdivision or branch line need be no more than a junction turnout, an interlocking tower and a foot or so of track disappearing offstage. You can model bitsa inter-

changes in much the same way—there's an example in the Small Town layout design on page 46. Scenically, a whole mountain range can be called into being by a few inches of nicely vertical rock face and a tunnel mouth.

Striking a track–scenery balance

On the current generation of large scenic model railroads, great emphasis is placed on the scenic setting—and a lot of space is devoted to creating it.

Often, much of this "decorative" scenery can use areas of the layout that are relatively dead in trackage potential: the inside of return curves or outside of corner tracks, peninsula ends, and those odd nooks and crannies result-

Structures on the Roque Bluffs layout serve as viewblocks to disguise tracks passing through the backdrop into staging.

Designing around a backdrop

The backdrop is the savior of the ever-cramped shelf layout, as it allows a scene to have real visual depth even when it's effectively only a narrow strip. A backdrop doesn't have to be elaborate to be effective, nor does it need to be a great work of art.

Often, something simple works best; painted scenery needs to complement the modeling, not compete with it. It also needs to use colors that match and blend with the modeling. These are the reasons I tend to shy away from pre-printed and photographic backscenes: they're often too detailed to live at the back of a small scene, while the colors rarely tally with those of scenic modeling materials. The backdrop is such a critical element of a shelf layout that I want to have as much control over it as possible.

Every railroad is different, so it's difficult to generalize about the best way of planning and executing a backdrop. Obviously, much will depend on how confident modelers feel with painting or whether they have any artistic friends who can be persuaded to work in exchange a refreshing beverage or two.

However, what I can suggest is that the backdrop should never be an afterthought. Quite the converse, it needs plenty of forethought at the planning stage, as it has a direct bearing on all other aspects of the layout design. Things you need to think about when planning a backdrop are, firstly, what you can convincingly represent on it, how you're going to support and light it, and how you're going to avoid unwanted cast shadows.

Backdrop content is the key factor. Obviously, the sky is a given and the most basic backdrops of all are unadorned sky scenes. Sometimes, that's all you need. To add hills and distant mountains is a matter of creating simple shapes and the proper restrained colors. Wooded hills and forests call for a bit more variegation in color and shape, while farmland is mostly a patchwork with subtle color variation between fields and perhaps the odd silo silhouetted against the sky.

ing from the architecture of the layout room. However, on a shelf layout such areas either don't exist in the first place, or have to be pressed into use to locate fundamental aspects of the railroad.

Almost always, any part of a shelf layout given over purely to scenery means a trade-off in trackage and hence operating potential. How we resolve the conflict of maximizing railroad interest while leaving room for realistic scenery is a fundamental factor in shelf layout planning.

Part of the answer to this one lies in your personal preferences and priorities. The conventional approach to layout design has always placed operating potential at the top of the pecking order, but there are plenty of modelers out there for whom intensive operation is not the over-riding priority.

Many folk, for instance, are more builders than operators, so creating a design incorporating plenty of interesting modeling challenges might well be a more important goal than squeezing in the last inch of running track or an extra industry spur. Several shelf layouts I've seen have been built to accommodate the simplest of all

operating patterns—merely allowing trains to circulate a continuous run, the point of the exercise being to re-create a lineside experience by just watching interesting, well-modeled equipment roll through a realistic setting.

The other part of the answer is to choose scenic subjects that can either be modeled in a small space or not modeled at all but represented on the backdrop. The first category centers around modeling features that are essentially vertical in nature; retaining walls, sheer rock faces, steep cut sides, trees, bushes and hedges, building fronts, lineside boundary fences and walls, and billboards. Low-relief modeling is an asset here, or combining a limited amount of relief modeling with complementary elements on the backdrop: paint the forest, but front it with just a few modeled trees.

The trick here is either to draw the eye away from or disguise the actual joint between the 3-D modeling and the flat-painted backdrop. I often try to design things so that such awkward transitions are hidden by foreground objects acting as view blocks—more on these in a moment.

The boatyard shed at left is used as a front-of-scene viewblock to divide the scene at Roque Bluffs into different areas of interest. The structure also helps disguise a section joint.

But buildings, industrial plants, rivers and canals, and linear elements like highways call for perspective drawing, something that is always difficult to achieve and which can only ever look right from one particular viewpoint. Unless you're well-versed in the rules of perspective and can arrange view blocks to confine the angles from which that part of the backdrop can seen, then I'd suggest that these are things best avoided. Ultimately, what you can feasibly include in the backdrop may well influence not just the things you can incorporate in the modeled scene and how they're placed, but just what you can choose to model in the first place!

Backdrop planning

The other things to avoid when planning a backdrop have to do with lighting. At the top of the list are those old chestnuts, sharp corners or angles in the plane of the backdrop and objects placed so they cast shadows on it.

Angular direction changes in a backdrop are impossible to hide, and serve only to destroy the illusion that the backdrop is there to create. Skies and distant scenery don't "do" corners

in the real world. If the backdrop must change direction, then curves—the gentler, the better—are far less obtrusive and much easier to light.

Thus I always plan my backdrops with coved corners—only needed in the horizontal plane where a valance is used to hide the upper extreme of the backdrop. I also try to avoid convex curves in backdrops, which are difficult (but not impossible) to light to kill the shape. From a lighting point of view, the ideal plan for a backdrop is a continuous convex curve, so that's what I always aim for.

It's one of the reasons why I prefer to divide the end of peninsulas into two separate scenes rather than trying to wrap scenery around a truncated backdrop. Well, when did you last see the end of the sky?

Avoiding giveaway cast shadows on the backdrop is all about working out the right relationship between the lighting, the objects casting the shadows (basically, any 3-D object in the scene, especially tall ones like line poles, trees, and structures), and the actual backdrop. Don't forget that this shadow-casting-object count should

include the trains. Nothing gives the game away quite like a shadowed silhouette pacing every train over the distant fields and sky.

Avoiding these unwanted shadows can be achieved in one of three ways, all which need to be considered at the planning stage: Often, careful placement of the shadow-casting object can do the trick. Objects placed in contact with the backdrop won't throw a shadow in the first place, while objects placed close to the backdrop in the right relation to the light source can hide their own shadows. At the other extreme, objects positioned well forward in the scene will cast shadows only on the modeled area, where they will simply look natural.

It's usually items in the middle of the modeled scene that cause problems, but by the nature of things, these are often unavoidable. So the second fix is to "catch" the unwanted shadow with a low-relief 3-D element such as a fence, billboard, wall, or simply vegetation, positioned immediately in front of the backdrop where the shadow falls.

Again, a cast shadow falling on the vertical face of a 3-D object doesn't

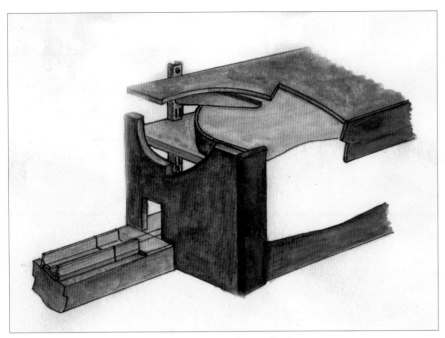

This diagram shows an end-of-scene viewblock with a "wing."

Exit stage left …

One of the visual factors that needs careful planning on a shelf layout employing hidden staging or fiddle yard tracks is the way the trains leave the modeled scenes—ideally in a natural or at least unobtrusive manner. Where the topography and situation permit them, bridges or tunnels are the traditional (and easiest) way to disguise such exits, but they're by no means a universal answer.

The railroad that apparently aims plumb-center for the only hill for miles around is a hoary old modeling chestnut; whether it's any worse than an undisguised "hole in the sky" exit through a backdrop is open to debate! In my book, neither is acceptable or unavoidable in the context of an eye-level-mounted shelf layout.

One of the many attractions of the natural viewpoint provided by eye-level display is that any object that would in reality obscure one's view of a train will do the same on the model—not the case with the helicopter view.

This opens up a whole range of possibilities by way of natural-looking ways for our trains to sneak offstage, as quite small features aptly placed can conceal the actual exit. Things like modest structures, minor pieces of topography, clumps of vegetation, fences, walls, billboards, and even strategically placed parked equipment, can be enough.

These view-blocking disguises can be varied and combined within a scene, particularly useful where several tracks have to sneak off into never-never land, as, for instance, when using the bitsa approach to suggest destinations rather then modeling them. Many of the designs presented later in this book use these sorts of devices; tunnels only appear where the accompanying mountains would be apt and truly immovable!

View blocks and viewpoints

There's a temptation when designing a shelf railroad to always keep the trackage "stage front" and to confine the scenic elements to the background.

Well, you certainly don't want to hide your railroad behind a forest of foreground clutter, but the occasional fence, structure, or landscape feature that briefly interrupts the view of the trains can be a useful design ploy. When carefully placed, such fore-

ground view blocks can divide the layout into several separate sub-scenes while hiding or diverting attention from things that—for any number of practical reasons—don't look quite right (unwanted shadows, for instance).

View blocks can also suggest particular viewpoints and steer the spectator away from certain locations, which can be helpful when you're trying to lose things like awkward perspectives around backdrop corners, joints between the model and the backdrop, and bits of necessary infrastructure that are better unseen.

Crafty use of view blocks to subdivide scenes can also give the impression that a train is travelling farther than it actually is, as the whole thing isn't always entirely visible and it passes a number of "events," a ploy that always seems to impart a sense of journey. Front-of-scene view blocks also help disguise the fact that our trains are usually way too short!

Side wings and end view blocks

Fortunately, viewing angles for shelf layouts are usually restricted anyway, unless you're one of those superheroes who can see through walls!

The kind of high-mounted shelf with a close-set top deck valance I'm suggesting here naturally invites face-on viewing from short range rather than encouraging the spectator to seek a long view down the length of the layout; shelf railroads never look convincing from that sort of an angle!

To cut out this unwanted viewing angle and to permit coved backdrop corners, I have long been an advocate of what I call "side wings," which along with the layout fascia and lighting valance, act to contain and frame the modeled scene and complete the shadow box. The way I arrange this for shelf layouts is shown in the sketch. As well as forming a visual frame the actual wing pieces serve to lose the end of the backdrop.

Just as the real sky has no top edge, it has no end either. So far, this is the best way I've come up with of terminating a backdrop in a natural way.

look unnatural the way it does on a 2-D drop. Where this isn't practicable, then you can move on to method three, killing thrown shadows with a wash of light from a source close to the top of the backdrop, as already outlined in Chapter 2.

CHAPTER FOUR

Portfolio

The proof of the pudding being in the eating, I've applied my suggested shelf layout design and constructional ideas to a portfolio of layout plans, ranging from an ultra-compact switching railroad housed in a bedroom closet to a medium-sized basement empire, and in scales ranging from N to O.

One of the author's track plans is in progress, being transformed from a line drawing to a watercolor illustration.

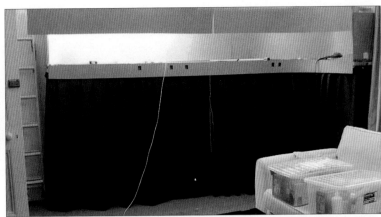

A detailed drawing with watercolor tinting is the author's preferred method of developing a final layout plan.

A well-designed shelf layout can complement any setting. This example is being built in a professorial study in one of the colleges at Oxford University.

Shelf layouts as a breed call for prototype railroad subjects that don't sprawl sideways, and one instance where that can never happen is when the railroad in question threads narrow, steep-sided valleys, crowding the banks of mountain rivers, or winding up the side creeks.

We've noted that the associated vertical scenery is also sparing of space—especially valuable when the shelf available for the model is on the narrow side. No surprise, then, that mountain railroading is prominent among these pages.

But it's not all hilly stuff. Other subjects include classic industrial switching, a Midwestern byway, New York car float operations, big-time railroading in downtown Chicago, a secondary main line in upper New York state, and a touch of California dreamin'. More variety than Heinz?

The one thing that's missing from the mix this time around, though, is big-time contemporary railroading. The generally compact nature of shelf layouts doesn't mix well with a prototype that seems to get bigger and longer and wider every time I look at it.

Although not specifically oriented toward small layouts, none of the plans drawn here could be described as large; the limitations of shelf format for wider footprints puts a limit on suitable subjects.

I've also been keen to take advantage of the plethora of new, high-quality ready-to-run models that have become available in recent times, most of which are historical in nature. Never

before has such a wonderful choice of mainline and backwoods steam power or charismatic first- and second-generation diesels been available. Many subjects that a few years ago could only have been modeled using costly brass engines and craftsman-built equipment are now accessible to everyone. These new possibilities are reflected in the designs showcased here.

All these layout proposals are sited in real domestic locations, most of which I've described in some detail. So my apologies to friends and family members who might be startled to find parts of their abodes figuring graphically in these pages.

Other examples use sites for which I've been asked to produce layout designs professionally. (The results shown here have nothing to do with the results of those commissions. I merely used the site—and accompanying problems—as a starting point for something completely different.)

To me, designing layouts in the abstract, without the discipline and restrictions of a real site, is a somewhat pointless exercise—hence my hi-jacking of actual locations. The German magazine MIBA (*Miniaturbahnen*) likes its layout designers to tailor their proposals to one of a series of standard sites based on the spaces and locations found in typical German houses. I always thought that a sound idea.

The plans mostly assume the use of track shelving for layout support with custom-made benchwork of the type suggested in Chapter 2. They are all intended to be close-lit with

under-the-shelf lighting systems and layout fascia and lighting valances as described.

I haven't been proscriptive as to control systems. Digital Command Control is always nice to have, but any of these designs would function perfectly well in conventional DC mode. Unless specifically mentioned in the notes accompanying the various plans, conventional knuckle couplers are envisioned, often used with magnetic or mechanical hand-picks for working the fiddle yards.

As is usual in my work, these are all hand-drawn plans, maybe lacking the ultimate precision, scale accuracy, and consistency of computer-generated artwork but, I like to think, possessed of a certain immediacy and character. The originals are in ink on fine-textured paper, tinted with watercolors, and drawn at scales of half, three-quarter, or inch to the foot. I believe what I draw is fairly unambiguous, but I do have a few quirky artwork conventions, as illustrated on the page facing. My overall aim is to try to convey an impression of the look, feel, and character of the design as well as the essential nuts and bolts.

Trackwork matters

A few words here about trackwork as drawn on these plans. Track is a fundamental aspect of any railroad, real or model, and as modelers, we have a wide choice of options.

At the most basic, we can use sectional track pieces of the type traditionally supplied with Christmas train

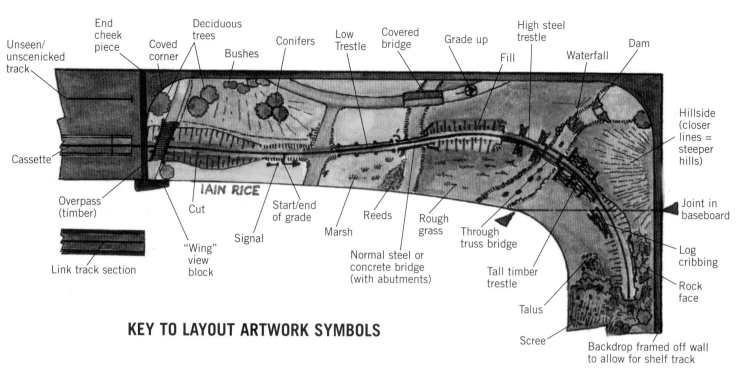

Unseen/unscenicked track · End cheek piece · Coved corner · Deciduous trees · Bushes · Conifers · Low Trestle · Covered bridge · Grade up · Fill · High steel trestle · Waterfall · Dam · Hillside (closer lines = steeper hills) · Cassette · Overpass (timber) · Cut · "Wing" view block · Signal · Start/end of grade · Marsh · Reeds · Rough grass · Normal steel or concrete bridge (with abutments) · Through truss bridge · Tall timber trestle · Talus · Scree · Joint in baseboard · Log cribbing · Rock face · Backdrop framed off wall to allow for shelf track · Link track section

IAIN RICE

KEY TO LAYOUT ARTWORK SYMBOLS

sets. Although such track works well enough and is certainly a great deal more realistic nowadays than it used to be, its ultra-tight curves, chunky rail cross-section, and fixed geometry are limiting in layout design terms.

At the other extreme, we can hand-lay all our track by spiking scale-size rail to accurately sized wooden ties, just like a full-size railroad. The result can look like a million dollars, and you can make any track arrangement or turnout formation you like, but at considerable cost in time, care, and effort (although not as much as you might think).

So most folks opt for the median choice of flextrack with pre-built turnouts, of which a huge choice is now available in a range of rail sizes and offering all manner of turnout numbers and types, together with diamonds and other complex formations.

Turnouts are the nub of all this. On both real railroads and models, they're classified by the frog numbers. This is a number derived from the angle of the frog vee expressed as a gradient. Thus, for a No. 6 turnout, the angle will be such that six feet back from the point of the frog (called the nose), the diverging rails will be one foot apart. For a No. 8, the one-foot divergence would be eight feet back from the nose —and so on. Simple enough.

However, it's a mistake to assume that all turnouts of a given frog number will be identical in overall dimensions

and geometry; far from it. There's a lot more to a turnout than just the frog, and the design and diverging angle of the switches and the length and form of the closure rails can vary considerably.

Most full-sized railroads had their own designs and practices. To pick a couple of examples for which I have prototype data in my library, a No. 8 turnout on the Maine Central is a very different beast from the same-named thing on the Missouri Pacific. The difference in lead (distance from the tips of the points to the nose of the frog) is a good eight feet longer on the MoPac, which works out to more than an inch in HO scale.

Well, here's a nice problem for layout designers, who are always being asked to nail everything down to the nearest millimeter on their published plans. I fear you just can't be that precise with regard to turnout geometry on a small-scale plan, especially a hand-drawn one. All you can do is to try your best to make sure that a No. 6 switch does indeed diverge at a 1-in-6 angle and is drawn to an appropriate length. Computers are much cleverer in this regard!

Given that the various ranges of ready-to-use turnouts vary fully as much in their geometry as do the MeC and the MoPac, you'll appreciate that a certain amount of leeway has to creep in. Yes, one could always specify that a given plan is suited only to Brand

X track, but that's very limiting both from the design and construction viewpoints—especially if you're a particular fan of Brand Y!

As a dyed-in-the-wool hand-spiker, I'm sometimes accused of not being sufficiently in tune with the restrictions of ready-to-use turnout geometries. This may be true in some cases.

If I'm thinking ready-to-lay, then Micro-Engineering or Peco are my usual choices. However, as far as possible, I seek to avoid turnout-geometry problems by erring on the too-long side in the drawing, with the thought that the worst result is an extra inch or two of plain track. However, I certainly can't rule out the need for tweaking should you choose to have a go at any of these designs.

It may be necessary to fiddle with a plan to fit a given range of track, maybe squeezing curves fractionally to find an extra inch of tangent, shifting spurs slightly, realigning, or shortening them. Or you can adjust things as you build, trimming turnouts to shorten them or even substituting an occasional item from a different maker.

Occasionally, you may need to go down a turnout number or nudge alignments so that a straight turnout can be made a into a wye, which is always shorter for the same frog angle. All of this is part of the rich tapestry of model railroading.

CHAPTER FIVE

The closet switching district (N scale)

Urban switching districts often feature street trackage winding among tall industrial buildings. Trains can serve a variety of businesses in a relatively small area. This 1980 scene shows Conrail operations in Detroit, Mich. *Byron Babbish*

Probably the most difficult type of home in which to find space for a model railroad is a rented apartment, especially if that railroad can't intrude in any way on the domestic use of the space.

The apartment for which this plan was conceived was one such—a compact two-bedroom, city bolthole 26 floors up in a tower overlooking the West River in Manhattan, a temporary home during a two-year work contract.

After the obvious places for model railroads had been ruled out, all that was left was a good-sized closet in the guest bedroom, a space two-and-a-half feet deep by six feet wide. Originally, this closet had three-piece sliding doors—no good at all for model railroad purposes. These were unhooked from their tracks and stored in a janitor's closet in the lobby. It pays to be on good terms with your building superintendent!

The doors were temporarily replaced by drapes matching those at the windows. These could be drawn to either side, leaving the closet as a handy-sized alcove in which to house an N scale switching layout.

Well, I can hear the groans from here: Oh no, not another compact switching puzzle! To which I'd reply: switching is the main form of operation on any model railroad, no matter what size. Even on the largest basement empire, simply running between towns is only a small part of the overall operating pattern. Apart from having the big-name passenger train high-tail through, main line running is pretty much the only major aspect of mainstream model railroading you can't enjoy on a layout schemed solely around switching.

In terms of construction and operating interest per square inch, few other types of model railroad can approach the entertainment potential of a well-planned, high-density switching scheme. Well-planned in this instance, of course, means the exact opposite of what a real railroad employee would understand by the term: awkward moves full of reversals, runaround tracks, see-saw set-backs, and grade crossings are grist to our mill rather than a right royal pain in the productivity!

Track and equipment

Switching puzzles like this are no easy option in constructional terms. Get-

Essential equipment for a switching district includes a switch engine and road- and transfer-service cabooses. A Canadian National SW1200 rests at Kitchener, Ont., in 1987. *Andrew Boyd*

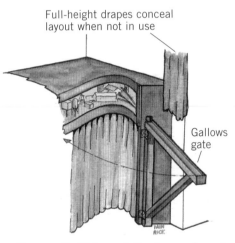

Full-height drapes conceal layout when not in use

Gallows gate

The cassette fiddle yard sits atop a swing-out gallows gate at one end of the layout. Drapes conceal the gate when folded.

A concrete batch plant will fit in well as a small industry served in the district.

ting a train to run steadily at speed on open, plain trackage with gentle curves is pretty much a no-brainer compared with achieving smooth, consistent, slow-speed, derailment-free, stop-start-reverse operation over tightly curved and convoluted trackwork with lots of close-spaced small-number turnouts.

Only the best standard of tracklaying and live-frog turnouts throughout will produce that kind of result. Although Micro-Engineering or Atlas new Code 55 are the best-looking N scale turnouts, for my money, only Peco has the range needed for this plan in the small rail size.

Similarly, locomotives will need top-flight mechanisms maintained in top-notch order. Rolling stock must track freely, with all the wheels accurately in gauge, properly and consistently weighted and—most importantly—with good couplers properly set up and working at 100-percent reliability.

All of this is a tall order in any scale but one that, not so long ago, would have been all-but-impossible in N scale. However, quality and refinement in this small size have improved in leaps and bounds, and today the best N scale equipment is on a par with its HO equivalents.

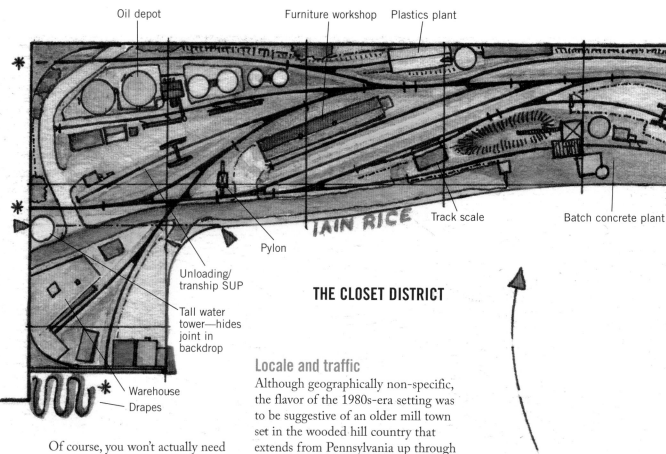

Oil depot   Furniture workshop Plastics plant

Track scale   Batch concrete plant

IAIN RICE

Pylon

Unloading/
tranship SUP

Tall water
tower—hides
joint in
backdrop

Warehouse
Drapes

THE CLOSET DISTRICT

Of course, you won't actually need
that much equipment for a layout like
this, although it can swallow up a surprising number and variety of freight
cars. That was part of the assignment
for me as the Micro-Trains N scale
car-collecting bug had well and truly
bitten! Locomotives came down to a
road switcher for working the interchange and two or three dedicated
switch engines.

My choices for the original concept, which centered around a typical industry zone on the fringes of a
medium-sized town somewhere in the
Northeast, were an Atlas GP38-2 in
Conrail blue (right for the period and
in keeping with the general location)
and a brace of miscellaneous switchers.

Unfortunately, N scale switchers
are not that thick on the ground even
today. Choices include the smooth-
running Kato EMD NW2 or the Alco
S1/S3 from Life-Like. My idea was
to choose models in fallen-flag paint
schemes, then blank out the old heralds
with paint patches and crudely re-letter
them to simulate second-hand locomotive purchases. But mainline railway
paint schemes—like the charismatic
Canadian National SW1200 illustrated—would also work well.

Locale and traffic

Although geographically non-specific,
the flavor of the 1980s-era setting was
to be suggestive of an older mill town
set in the wooded hill country that
extends from Pennsylvania up through
New Jersey, New York, and New England into the Canadian border area.

The industries and associated structures included are totally unremarkable.
When trying to create a convincing but
fictional location, I always find it pays
to use highly typical, everyday elements
to make up the scene.

So here we have a selection of
favorites, intended to justify a range
of different car types: a batch concrete
plant (covered hoppers of cement and
hoppers of quarry products); a furniture
mill (forest products in by center-beam
flats, finished products out by boxcars
or containers); a plastics facility (pellets
in by covered hoppers, moldings out
in boxcars); a fuel depot handling oil
products and LPG (tank cars), a cold-
storage warehouse (mechanical reefers),
and a salvage and recycling facility
(gondolas and flats of scrap, boxcars of
baled paper).

For any car not thus catered for,
there's always the car repair facility.
To house and maintain those essential
switch engines, there's a small metal
enginehouse with a refuelling facility.
Any lading checks can be made with
the track scale included on the run-
around track. Non-railroad facilities

include the essential roadside diner;
mine are easy-over, thanks…

Inspiration for these industries and
the buildings they use have come from
all over, although both of the facilities
illustrated here were snapped in the
upper Midwest. With these industries,
you tend to find similar structures serving just about anywhere in the U.S.

Changing the scenic background,
signs, main line, railroad connection, and the type of lighting could
place this ordinary scene just about
anywhere.

And as for the structures—straightforward kitbashing and kitmingling
should provide all you need, unless
structures are your thing, in which case
scratchbuilt models of actual prototypes would be nice.

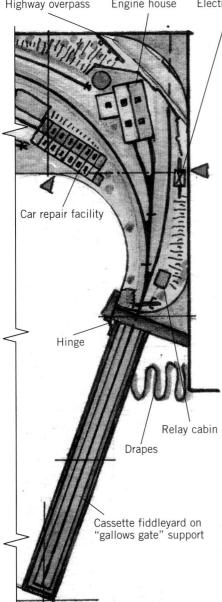

Highway overpass   Engine house   Electrical box—hides joint in backdrop

Car repair facility

Hinge

Relay cabin

Drapes

Cassette fiddleyard on "gallows gate" support

The operators would also want to be pretty close friends.

Construction

This is a straightforward design. With little topography to account for, the benchwork should be fairly flat and simple. There's one main shelf six feet long by a little over a foot at the widest, with two small sub-shelves measuring about a foot-and-a-half long and six or twelve inches long; all are portable.

End view blocks ease portability, and I envisioned the backdrop being attached to the baseboards rather than being supported off the wall. It's only ten inches tall, after all, so the "cracks in the sky" can be disguised by a tall water tank and an electricity line tower.

The only real complexity is the light-weight "gallows leg" which swings out to support the cassette fiddle yard. This is hinged from a vertical stud screwed to the upper (top deck) and lower (layout)

shelves and carried down to the floor as in the sketch on the plan. The gallows lies inside the line of the drapes when the railroad is not in use, and takes the form of a plain shelf surrounded by a low fence to hold the cassettes securely. Extra cassettes are stored on a service shelf below the layout.

The layout and its location in the closet were conceived as a temporary arrangement, with the idea that these boards would form the nucleus of a larger and more-permanent layout at a later time. For this reason, the actual track plan was designed to be readily extended in just about any direction using the tracks leaving the scene at points marked with an asterisk, as well as the lead to the fiddle yard.

In the meantime, the railroad could offer some straightforward but rewarding construction projects and entertaining operation; just the thing after a long, hard day at the office.

Operation

Wherever you choose to locate the Closet District, operation will be much the same. Cuts of cars will be brought in from the mainline "interchange" (the cassette fiddle yard), broken down, and then spotted as required at the various industries, exchanging loads for empties or vice-versa.

A computer- or card-based traffic system could give shape and challenge to these workings by generating traffic flows and their accompanying car requirements. You could make things pretty intensive, with two engines at work at the same time, although ideally that would call for DCC to avoid a lot of tedious electrical block switching.

Rail-served bulk oil dealers can be found across the country, and the tanks, structures, and fittings offer a great deal of modeling and detail potential.

CHAPTER SIX

The small town on the prairie (HO scale)

You can capture the feel of a railroad in the Midwest, with its fields, rolling hills, and small towns, in a fairly small area. Here a Chicago, Burlington & Quincy train heads westward toward Buda, Ill., in the early 1940s. *Ira H. Eigsti*

A common starter model railroad is a tabletop layout, traditionally built on a 4 x 8-foot sheet of half-inch construction plywood in HO or on a lightweight panel door (2½ x 6½ feet) in N.

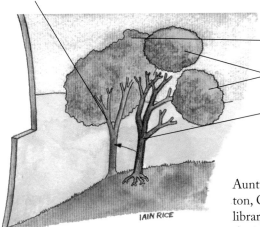

Branches (with or without trunk) painted on backdrop (trunk must match 3-D outline)

Foliage painted on backscene—color matched to 3-D foliage

3-D foliage clumps: poly-fiber with ground foam or foliage mat

Plastic, twisted-wire, or natural material 3-D tree armature—sand flat on back to get a good fit with backscene

IAIN RICE

Low-relief trees combine painting part of the tree on the backdrop with 3-D modeling for foreground foliage and branches.

But such tabletops are only workable as layout sites if you have a big enough room to house them with a reasonable-width aisle around at least three sides of the table (two long sides and an end). Two feet of clearance between the table and the wall is about the practical minimum, with a yard being far more comfortable.

All of which means that your "compact" HO railroad actually needs a space of at least 8 x 10 feet, or 8 x 12 feet to access all four sides. And that will need to be dedicated space, as even pushed into a corner, such a layout will take up so much available area that what's left can't be used for other purposes. Tabletop railroads have never struck me as being very space-efficient in this regard as the modeling area (32 square feet) is only a third of the area exclusively needed to house it.

In larger homes with basements or multi-car garages, coming up with a spare 8 x 12 corner for a railroad is no big deal. However, in a townhouse, trailer-home, city apartment, retirement condominium, or in many smaller traditional homes, finding 96 square feet for dedicated model railroad use is not so easy.

Many such compact homes have rooms no bigger than that—rooms that will need to be slept in, studied in, or at least shared with other hobby and domestic activities. Such rooms are like the "back room" in my

Aunt Nancy's old house in Kingston, Ontario. Sometime study, studio, library, office, store, the place to set up the ironing board, somewhere to escape to when there were too many visiting relatives clogging up the house, it may have been the most essential space in the whole house.

I suspect there are a lot of rooms like the one at Aunt Nancy's—with the door in one shorter wall and a window in the other, the odd closet or desk, and shelves right around most of the walls—pretty much floor to ceiling.

All you need to build this modest model railroad, which is the shelf equivalent of a traditional 4 x 8 in terms of content and scope, is just one of those shelves around four-and-a-half feet from the floor, a foot-and-a-half wide along one long wall, considerably less around the others, with a couple of simple lift-out link sections bridging the doorway and window.

What you get from this site is a modeling area quite a bit smaller than the 32 square feet of the 4 x 8 table—say, around 24 square feet. However, it's all usable railroad right-of-way with no dead areas, permitting a much longer run than on any 4 x 8 and allowing wider curves, longer trains, and bigger equipment. And this around-the-walls 8 x 12 shelf site offers all that while having a minimal impact on the room, which can still fulfill many other functions.

The only real problem is what you do about the door, as this will almost certainly open into the room and conflict with the railroad's right-of-way. There are three solutions: Re-hang the door so it opens outward, replace it with a folding or sliding door that does not impinge on the room, or do

away with it altogether and just have an open doorway, maybe with a bead curtain or draw-aside drape.

Small but oh-so-beautiful

So what we have here is a modest model railroad planned around the ultimate shelf right-of-way—long but mostly thin, with not a great deal of space for scenery. You could look at this as a recipe for an almost-instant model railroad—just grab a few yards of flex-track, a handful of turnouts and a selection of ready-built or shake-the-box structures, and fling the thing together over a rainy weekend.

Many a 4 x 8 layout comes into being just like that. But just because it's modest in scope doesn't mean a model railroad has to be modest in ambition. My take on this sort of minimal model railroad goes like this: If there's not a whole lot to look at, what is seen had better be good. It's about quality over quantity, about making every detail and object count. Here's a chance to strive for better standards and to aim for super-smooth operation, ultimate realism, and convincing atmosphere.

In this case, the chosen subject (an old favorite) is a secondary route somewhere out in the farming states of the upper Midwest, set in those transition years between black-and-white and Kodachrome—say, anywhere between 1940 and 1955. Prototype railroad inspirations could include the Chicago & North Western, Burlington Route, Illinois Central, Monon, Minneapolis & St. Louis, Milwaukee Road, Soo Line, or perhaps a freelanced granger short line.

Low-relief trees highlight the author's British-prototype Trerice layout.

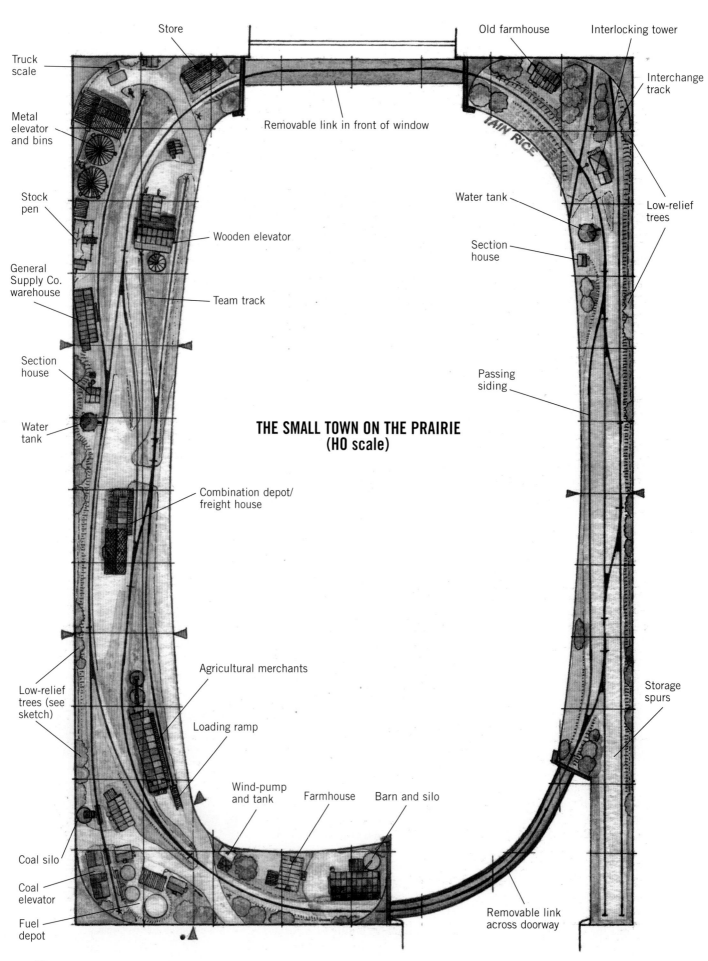

Truck scale

Store

Old farmhouse

Interlocking tower

Metal elevator and bins

Interchange track

Removable link in front of window

Stock pen

Water tank

Low-relief trees

Section house

Wooden elevator

General Supply Co. warehouse

Team track

Section house

Water tank

**THE SMALL TOWN ON THE PRAIRIE
(HO scale)**

Passing siding

Combination depot/ freight house

Agricultural merchants

Low-relief trees (see sketch)

Storage spurs

Loading ramp

Wind-pump and tank

Farmhouse

Barn and silo

Coal silo

Coal elevator

Fuel depot

Removable link across doorway

My interest in this type of theme and timeframe has been inspired by those classic, gritty railroad and social images produced by the generation of documentary photographers who emerged in the later 1930s: Marion Post Wolcott, Arthur Rothstein, Russell Lee, Dorothea Lange, John Vachon, Charles Clegg, Jack Delano, and O. Winston Link. Try *An American Journey*, edited by Mark Vandercook (Hotbox Press, 2000; ISBN 0-9703544-4-4) for the flavor.

Complementary to this pioneering monochrome work are the early color slides taken by post-war railfans like Dick Wallin, George Lloyd, and Jim Buckley. All these pictures have sharp detail and tangible atmosphere by the bucketful—and that's exactly what gets my modelling juices flowing.

The layout features an archetypal Midwestern small-town railroad station, a combination depot (that's a passenger station with an integral freight house) sitting on the main and a loop/house track/switching lead running around the back.

The station agent has his office and telegraph key in this building, with a train order semaphore perched above the roof. Adjacent to the depot is a short team track for general lading. On the far side of the main, there's a water tank and a section house for the local track maintenance crew. And so far as the railroad goes, that's about it.

Everything else is spurs serving the essentials of the town and the farming community, starting with the all-important grain elevators. Two, in this case—a newer, metal-sheathed affair for the railroad's shippers grain line, the other the traditional timber-frame pattern belonging to the local farmer's co-operative, iconic structures, 35,000 bushels or so in capacity, with a few thousand more in the characteristic form of cylindrical corrugated-metal "Butler bins."

Next comes the agricultural merchant and implement dealer, supplying farm necessities of all sorts: seed, fertilizer, fencing materials, tools, hardware, veterinary supplies, and animal feeds. At the end of their spur, there's an unloading ramp for vehicles arriving on

Iconic structures of the American plains include small wood-framed depots and grain elevators ("prairie skyscrapers"). *William S. Christopher*

flatcars—a handful of new Farmalls or John Deeres each season, but mostly used equipment.

Another essential lineside industry is the fuel dealer, holding stocks of farm diesel, gasoline, kerosene, domestic coal, and heating oil—it can get mighty cold around these parts in the dark months of the year. Other trackside facilities include a livestock ramp and pens and a supply depot that keeps the goods on the shelves of the town's stores.

The station and the fringes of the town, represented by a traditional farmstead and a solitary store to suggest the end of main street, occupy the main shelf, which has a mean width of 18 inches or so. I'd make this benchwork in three handy four-foot sections that would be small enough to work on at a bench or even on the kitchen table, with a fourth smaller board for the farm on the approach from the doorway.

On the opposite long wall is a much narrower shelf, mostly about 10 inches wide, which contains a second scene that also acts as the layout's staging and fiddle yard. I normally would place these elements in a hidden or offstage location, but in a small room-based layout like this, there's not really any place to hide. A bare staging yard right along one main wall is hardly too exciting to look at, hence the notion of "scenic staging." The only truly offstage trackage is the pair of spurs right alongside the doorway. Of these, the shorter is

intended to hold the "varnish"—a Ten-Wheeler and a couple of passenger cars—while the longer will take the branch freight: a 2-8-0, six cars, and a caboose.

To justify the spurs, passing siding, and loop, I've based this simple scene, which has hardly any scenery, on that other classic Midwestern railroad element, a flat crossing with another railroad (dummy) with interchange (semi-working). See the "bitsa" scene as proposed in Chapter 3.

Here, there's an interlocking tower guarding the crossing, with a water tank and section house completing the railroad facilities. With the passing siding and using the interchange track for further parking, the layout thus has the capacity to handle at least four discrete trains.

Add that to mainline curves at a "big layout" 30-inch or greater radius and no turnout tighter that a No. 6, and this simple shelf empire packs quite a fair potential. I fancy it offers more interesting operation and visual realism than any 4 x 8 table-top.

Midwestern recipe needs quality ingredients

Atmosphere and detail are great ingredients for any model railroad, but the Midwestern theme brings a few other dishes to the table (or shelf, in this case).

Capturing the essence of the rural Midwest doesn't call for masses of

Many branch lines and secondary mains were served by mixed trains, as seen on the Milwaukee Road's branch to Mineral Point, Wis., in the 1950s. The track on these lines tended to meander more and feature more weeds than on main lines. *Paul Larson*

rockwork, acres of industrial plant, whole city blocks, or forests of trees. What it does demand is quality and subtlety. The landscape may be big in terms of tall skies and wide open spaces—but it's small in terms of detail. Capturing the slight changes in level, the berms and banks, the fences and ditches, and the characteristic vegetation calls for a keen eye and skilled modeling.

Those all-important shade trees may be relatively few in number, but each one will need to be an individual model rather than a simple ball of poly fiber and ground foam. In the context of this shelf design, I've used "half-relief" trees; the sketch on page 45 shows how I make these. Color also needs to be carefully observed and reproduced. Study the wonderful work of Lance Mindheim for an object lesson in this art.

Similarly, the handful of structures found trackside will need to be true to prototype, carefully modeled, and especially well weathered. For this is a land with an unkind—often savage—climate. Post-Depression, there weren't many spare dollars floating around for new siding or fresh paint.

At this period, many structures were in a pretty parlous state, so there's almost infinite scope for making use of subtle distressing and weathering treatments. It doesn't much matter if you start with plastic kits, go the craftsman kit route, or don the hair-shirt and embark on some board-by-board

scratchbuilding, what you need to finish with are models that reward the closest inspection.

With relatively few things to build, you can take the time to produce something special in each case, something individual and full of character. Maybe you'll want to do this in two stages, perhaps starting out with a straightforward kitbuilt structure as a placeholder while you take the time to research and build a better model.

Of course, it's no good having ultra-realistic landscape or blow-your-socks-off structures if the railroad itself isn't up to snuff. Not so long ago you'd have been trawling the brass ads and busting into the piggy-bank for the locomotives and rolling stock to equip a layout like this. Not any more.

The current generation of ready-to-run die-cast and plastic locomotives and cars offers all you need, and to a standard to match even the best of settings. In the HO scale envisioned for this plan, half a dozen items of inexpensive motive power would sit at the top of my shopping list: Bachmann's generic Ten-Wheeler and 2-8-0 for steam, the Atlas Alco RS-1 and an EMD Geep or SD7 or SD9 for first-generation diesel power, and Bachmann's gas-electric doodlebug to handle the passengers and mail.

For the trains to go behind the power, there are literally hundreds of suitable freight cars to choose from. Only if your taste runs to a spot of

varnish do you hit snags—older and shorter wood-body or heavyweight steel passenger cars not being that plentiful on dealer's shelves. But for a layout like this, a combine and a coach or two is all you'll need. There are some neat resin kits out there for older passenger equipment, and they're not that difficult to build!

Which only leaves the track. A railroad like this would lose a lot of its down-home character if you laid it in deep-ballasted heavyweight track; irregular ties, light rail, and gravel or cinder ballast is more like it. In these hard times, maintenance is at a minimum, so the alignment and "top" (how level the rails were) would probably be none too good. Even the main line would be well-endowed with weeds, and sidings and spurs would carry a fair crop of hay! Handlaid track would be a natural for this, but Micro-Engineering's code 70 flextrack and turnouts would do the job almost as well. Use the lighter code 55 flextrack for the spurs. There's a curved turnout on the approach by the fuel depot—a Shinohara No. 326 right-hand code 70 turnout should fit the bill—and the fuel depot turnout itself is a No. 8. All the rest are straightforward No. 6 switches.

Weather the track well and ballast with Woodland Scenics cinders and fine brown stone. Add a good sprinkling of acrylic fiber and ground-foam grass and weeds, and you should get the right run-down look.

CHAPTER SEVEN

Elm Point (HO scale)

In 2004 I spent quite a few weeks in New York City, as part of a team working on a number of layout projects around the Big Apple. One of these jobs was located over the Hudson in the Palisades area of New Jersey, which involved a long commute from our base in Queens. That commute often took us along the Bruckner Expressway and over the Tri-Boro Bridge, with its great view of the New Haven's mighty Hell Gate arch, one of the world's more impressive structures. Well, Bruckner was an expressway in name only; most of the time it was frozen with congestion.

The New York, New Haven & Hartford had an extensive series of docks for car floats at Oak Point in New York City. *NYNH&H*

A New Haven tugboat guides two car floats under the Triborough bridge on its way to the docks at Oak Point. Each float could carry about 20 40-foot cars. *Alfred F. Tyrrill*

The commute gave me plenty of time to get acquainted with the maze of railroad tracks beside and below the elevated highway. A long, narrow yard full of freight cars parallels the four-track electrified main, with spurs going off hither and thither along the banks of the old Bronx Kill toward the Harlem River at the south end. A raft of stub tracks turns southward by the Leggett Avenue overpass to the north—spurs that ran down to dead-end on the bank of the East River.

This complex, I soon learned, was the legendary Oak Point, northernmost terminal of the fabled New York Harbor car float operations. Those tracks dead-ending on the riverbank had formerly served a series of docks with transfer bridges to link with the car floats, each of which had three tracks and could carry 15 or 18 cars. Pairs of these floats sandwiched a tall tugboat of the New Haven's marine department for the long haul beneath Hell Gate, down the East River, and around the tip of Manhattan, before mingling with the ocean-goers in the wide waters of New York Harbor for the trek across to the Jersey shore. The destination was Greenville Yard and a connection with the Pennsy.

This somewhat laborious operation mostly handled traffic to and from the immediate east New York area and southern Connecticut. Through freight headed south to Pennsylvania and western New Jersey from farther north on the New Haven system, turned west at Derby Junction, Conn., and threaded the Mountain Division to Maybrook Yard in New Jersey, crossing the Hudson by the mighty high steel span at Poughkeepsie. Maybrook was shared with the NH's southern and western partners: the Erie, Lehigh & Hudson River, Lehigh & New England, and the wandering New York, Ontario & Western.

Oak to Elm

So much for reality. I've made several attempts at designing prototypical layouts based on Oak Point (which is still an active facility, now owned by CSX), but the whole thing sprawls far too much to form a workable basis for a compact model railroad. No way would it fit on any sort of shelf!

So I've pulled my usual trick of stealing elements of the prototype and combining them in a completely fictional way—an approach I term composite layout design. The result

is a U-shaped HO shelf system that I've christened Elm Point. Here, the purloined elements are the car float terminal itself, the small yard serving it, and a bunch of industry tracks taking off to thread the streets and river banks of the South Bronx.

There's also a switch-engine stabling and servicing facility and lots of signature New York urban wasteland elements—elevated highways, big billboards, characteristic industrial structures, stained and crumbling concrete retaining walls, areas of exposed rock, pockets of waste ground, and plenty of junk. Fascinating and historic though it is, no one ever described this part of the South Bronx waterfront as beautiful.

Elm Point is, of course, a far smaller and more modest facility than Oak, but they have some specific characteristics in common, most notably the squeezed-in location that occupies a narrow strip of foreshore between major highways and industrial buildings and the riverbank. Several highways and buildings are located partly over the railroad tracks on massive, heavily riveted elevated steel structures. This is almost a real "railroad in the basement."

By contrast, not in the basement but on a brief section of elevated right-of-way, is a little segment of NYT subway track. Could it be a hitherto-unsuspected loop of the Lexington Avenue line's No. 6 route out to Pelham?

Anyway, it's an excuse to have a short four-car subway train—perhaps on a timer—rattle past from time to time. Yes, I know subway tracks are normally double, but at the elevated viewing height at which this layout is set, the subway tracks are pretty much on eye level, so the lack of a second track is not too apparent. The single track keeps things simple on what is effectively background animation.

Elm Point Yard itself is tightly packed, with sharp curves, short spurs, short-number turnouts, and complex formations including a double-slip compound and a three-way turnout. I had Peco's code 75 Fine Scale ready-made turnouts in mind here. The main line is carried right through, appearing and disappearing from beneath highways to give the impression of continuity. It's actually stub ended; the south end doesn't go anywhere and simply acts as a switching lead. At the north end, the main makes a hidden 90-degree turn beneath the elevated highway and subway tracks as soon as it is off scene, sneaking behind the car float dock to reach a cassette fiddle yard.

Cassettes and car-floats

This fiddle yard is one of the less-usual aspects of the design, as it takes the form of a removable shelf spanning the window. This is a ploy I've used on several occasions when space is tight, taking advantage of the fact that a cassette fiddle yard needs no fixed trackage beyond the matching lead-in section, which only need be a couple of inches long (see page 20 in Chapter 2).

In this instance, this fixed lead is incorporated in the end few inches of the hidden mainline track where it emerges through the end view-blocking "wing piece" adjacent to the car float dock. Thus, all that is needed to support the cassettes used to receive and re-marshal trains is a plain shelf—a five-and-a-half-foot-long plank some four inches wide, sitting on a support ledge on the wing piece of the layout, and on a simple and unobtrusive small bracket on the far side of the window. The window in this case uses blinds rather than conventional drapes.

The only other unusual feature of the design is the use of the car floats to form part of the off-scene staging for the layout. Loaded floats are undocked and moved out from the transfer bridge before being slid off of the corner of the layout as shown. Then they're carefully lifted down to storage on shelving beneath the layout in much the same way as cassettes are used to handle equipment in fiddle yards.

I've designed my floats to be a size smaller than the New Haven's big three-track jobs, making them shorter (still a bit over 200 feet—about 28 inches in HO) and with two tracks only. They're capable of holding ten 40-foot cars or eight 50-footers.

The cars are held in place on the floats very simply. At the outboard end of each float track is a removable restraint post carrying a fixed knuckle coupler with no trip pin. These posts, which I'd make from K&S square-section telescopic brass tube, would be simply lifted out vertically from their sockets when the float is in position at the transfer bridge, thus disengaging them from the couplers on the cars.

Ultimate office accessory?

The projected site for this small slice of the Big Apple is one long wall and most of the ends of a 9½ x 16-foot room, part of a modest single-floor house extension in the Netherlands. The original is used as an architect's home office.

A removable bumper post for a car float can be made from pieces of brass tubing with a Kadee coupler mounted on top.

There are sliding glass doors and a pair of tall-but-narrow windows in the opposite long wall to the layout, with a work station and traditional drawing board in front of them. The door to the rest of the house is in one corner, but the remainder of the room is blessedly free from built-in obstructions.

This layout proposal—one of several for this site—is designed to sit with the track at a higher-than-usual 60 inches above floor level, integrated with bookshelves and filing cabinets (one reason for the display height), storage drawers and cupboards, a large-screen TV, and an audio system. However, the basic design could be readily adapted to fit a small basement, a bedroom, or part of a one-car garage. I rather like the high-level display, with it's duck's-eye view of the waterfront.

To fit in with this location, careful design was needed to marry the footprint and presentation of the layout to the various objects and items of furniture beneath it. Thus, for instance, the wide shelf section carrying the car float dock is matched to the pair of filing cabinets that live in this corner of the room, conveniently giving a generous 30 inches of depth to this part of the scene.

This wide shelf, which being mostly water is of relatively light construction, is supported by 24-inch shelf track brackets on the end wall rather than resting on top of the 56-inch high cabinets. This may seem illogical until you consider the jolt with which heavily laden file drawers can slam home, quite enough to affect the layout if it were physically connected to the cabinets. Overturned boxcars floating down the East River weren't part of the proposed operating scheme, even if not entirely unprototypical.

Storage for extra cassettes and the spare car floats is arranged beneath the tug dock, integral with the custom-built office storage cabinets occupying this location. The TV and audio system live beneath the yard, with the two large monitor loudspeakers situated beneath the slightly wider ends. They are angled toward the listening position at the work station and aligned precisely with the gentle curve of the layout fascia—the sort of design detail that architects just love, and which can be so important when integrating a layout into a domestic or business setting.

Similarly, the top and bottom layout fascias were intended to be veneered, stained a trendy blue-gray shade and satin-varnished to match the finish of the room's custom cabinetry. All very smart.

Equipment

Oak Point was a New Haven facility, and so is Elm—although you could sneak in a bit of New York Central or Long Island Rail Road equipment

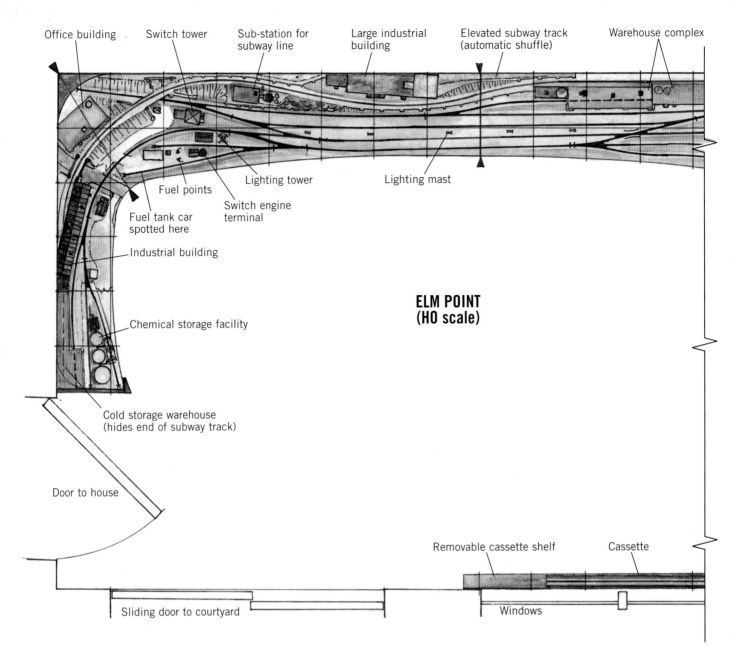

Office building　Switch tower　Sub-station for subway line　Large industrial building　Elevated subway track (automatic shuffle)　Warehouse complex

Lighting tower　Lighting mast

Fuel points

Switch engine terminal

Fuel tank car spotted here

Industrial building

Chemical storage facility

ELM POINT
(HO scale)

Cold storage warehouse (hides end of subway track)

Door to house

Removable cassette shelf　Cassette

Sliding door to courtyard　Windows

without stretching things too far. Having the NH as the key player is a decision based not just on prototype conformity, but also on the attractive and varied switching power rostered by the railroad during this period, which included USRA 0-8-0 steam switchers and a selection of pioneer diesels.

The New Haven was a very early user of diesel-electric switchers—which they classed as DEY (diesel-electric yard). Types tried included Alco's pioneering 1931-built 600-hp prototype (DEY-1), "trialed" on the NH, followed by a fleet of 1936-vintage GE 600-hp units (DEY-2). In 1938 came the more powerful 660-hp DEY-1b Alco HH660 switchers. For the lightest work, the NH stuck with GE's ubiquitous 44-tonner.

For everything bigger, Alco initially won out, with the road buying a total of 65 S-3s and 22 S-2s before General Motors muscled in on the scene in 1956, supplying a fleet of EMD's meaty 1200-hp SW1200 switchers. For the 1940s era envisioned for this plan, steam and Alcos would hold sway, aided by a 44-tonner or two.

Proto 2000 and Atlas have both listed the Alco S-2 and S-3 switchers, and Bachmann the GE 44-tonner; however, these ready-to-run models are usually offered in the later green-and-orange or in McGinnis-era black, white and red. The earlier plain green or green/orange "script" paint schemes will probably call for the airbrush and decals. Atlas now makes an Alco HH660 in plastic.

The early GE 600-hp switchers were a boxcab design, so you might be able to find an old Roundhouse boxcab diesel kit as a starting point. These distinctive early oil-electrics were extensively used for New York car float operations by all the other main participating railroads: Jersey Central, LIRR, Pennsy, and NYC.

Suitable NH steam power is available in the Proto 2000 Heritage series: The USRA 0-8-0 has been listed as a NH 3400-series, while the 0-6-0 would not be out of place. The odd road diesel could also put in an appearance, with the Proto 1000 Alco RS-2 being the most likely candidate.

On the elevated subway tracks, a four-car set of Life-Like's Proto 1000 R21/R22 New York subway cars would

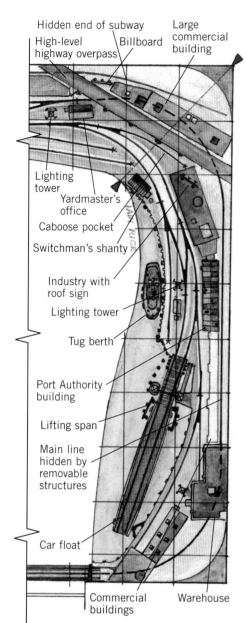

Hidden end of subway
Large commercial building
High-level highway overpass
Billboard
Lighting tower
Yardmaster's office
Caboose pocket
Switchman's shanty
Industry with roof sign
Lighting tower
Tug berth
Port Authority building
Lifting span
Main line hidden by removable structures
Car float
Commercial buildings
Warehouse

The New Haven owned several pioneering Alco HH-series diesel switchers, along with early GE 600-hp units and later models from Alco, GE, and EMD. *NYNH&H*

fit quite nicely, although technically they would be a little bit out of period, as both series actually date from the mid-1950s. In the context of this scheme, either the charismatic round-window Redbirds or the slightly plainer dark green R22s would certainly create the right impression. A pair of R22s were NYT's first unmanned automatic train, so having a train of them shuttle back and forth under the control of an automatic reversing module with timer would seem quite appropriate!

Judging from photographic evidence, the vast majority of car float traffic traveled in boxcars and reefers, with just the odd tank car, mill gondola, or flat. But the industries at the south end could offer more variety: covered hoppers, gons or hoppers of coal, fuel oil or chemicals in tanks, and machinery or bulky items on heavy flats or in gons. Other possible traffic might include lumber and building supplies, aggregates, metal feedstocks, refrigerated perishables, and scrap metal or other industrial trash. There would also need to be fuel and sand for the railroad's own power, plus the odd piece of maintenance-of-way equipment. The yard capacity is not that great, so a huge choice of equipment would not be needed.

Scenery and structures

We're talking urban wasteland here—although when I first came to New York I was surprised at just how much green open space there is in areas like the South Bronx. In terms of this railroad-heavy layout, though, scenery amounts to little more than a few patches of rough grass and weeds and a bit of exposed rock.

Far more significant are the structures. Here's a chance to kitbash a motley collection of mostly industrial buildings of different ages, with signature New York rooflines. Is there some New York city ordinance that says you have to put as many things as possible up there? Water tanks, air conditioning plant, elevator hoists, ventilation and dust extraction equipment, chimneys, piping, and—of course—advertising signs are all part of the New York roofscape. The other signature structure detail is the spindly iron fire escape draped

down every building side; fortunately, Walthers has them in its Cornerstone series. In fact, pretty much everything you need is out there from DPM, Great West Models, Rix, Pikestuff, Walthers, and a host of small suppliers.

Operation

When the various New York car float operations were in full swing, they together handled more than 2,000 car movements in a 24-hour period. Aside from the intensive car float traffic, Elm Point is a straightforward waterfront and industrial switching railroad.

It's designed around relatively short—six cars or so—transfer runs, which enter the compact four-track classification yard from the cassette fiddle yard at the south end. Arriving trains are broken down by the dedicated yard switcher, with the caboose being tucked away in the "cabin pocket" nestled in the shadow of the elevated highway on tall steel stilts that dominates and disguises the right-hand corner of the scene. Cuts of cars ready to cross the harbor to the Jersey shore would be assembled in the pair of stub-end spurs adjacent to the car float lead track, and switched onto the float with the use of an idler flat or two—a job for a second dedicated switch engine.

Other than that, it's just straightforward industrial switching against a distinctive New York background, with the occasional distraction as a subway train rolls and rattles by.

CHAPTER EIGHT

White Mountain logger
(HO scale)

East Branch & Lincoln No. 5, now at the White Mountain Central Railroad in Lincoln, N.H., is an example of a Baldwin saddletank locomotive common to New England logging railroads. *Richard Jenkins/White Mountain Central*

Mention New Hampshire's White Mountains to railroad buffs and two words spring to mind: Crawford Notch. The Maine Central's long, twisting grade from Bartlett up the headwaters of the Saco River to the famous mountain pass is legendary in railroad lore. Even dyed-in-the-wool Santa Fe fans have heard of it!

Far less well-known, however, are the tortuous logging lines that also once threaded these steep-shouldered hills—17 in all, connected to the Boston & Maine around Lincoln to the west, to the Grand Trunk at West Milan and Berlin in the north, and along the length of the MeC's Mountain Division, taking off up the Saco's side-valleys into the steep New Hampshire forests.

Every death-defying stunt pulled by better-known Pacific Northwest logging railroads had an echo in these Eastern mountains: twisting rights-of-way along ledges carved from near-vertical hillsides, grades that seemingly defied gravity, curves tight enough to squeeze your eyes closed, and tall fills barely wide enough to support the tie-ends.

The New Hampshire log trains—rattling and reeling along behind their diamond-stacked Portland four-wheelers and Baldwin 2-4-2 saddle-tankers or toiling upgrade under gear-grinding Shay or Climax power—tiptoed over teetering trestles, see-sawed up switchbacks, and squealed around spirals. For four months of the year, they were battling the deep snow of New England winters before suffering sudden washouts from spring thaws. The long summers were spent in fear of the terrible consequences of a stray spark in the wrong place.

Some of these White Mountain timber operations were connected to the long fingers of the immortal Maine two-foot railroads, reaching in from the coastal plains to the foot of the big hills; logs from the fringes of the high forest rolled out over the farthest reaches of this narrow-gauge iron—by the remote, lonely Monson or by the better-connected Phillips & Rangeley, Eustis, and Franklin & Megantic railroads—all northward branches from the trunk of the Sandy River & Rangeley Lakes.

But here, it's the standard-gauge logging roads of the White Mountains proper I'm interested in: roads with names like the Irish-sounding Lancaster & Kilkenny, the rumbustious Wild River RR, the remote and short-lived Upper Ammonoosuc, the substantial Zealand Valley RR, and the long-lasting East Branch & Lincoln, which ran for more than half a century and lingered

until 1948. You've probably never heard of most of these roads; I know I hadn't, until I found sitting on a second-hand book-dealer's shelf *Logging Railroads of the White Mountains*. Written by C. Francis Belcher and published in 1980 by the Appalachian Mountain Club, the ISBN is 0-910146-32-2, if you want to track down a copy.

This little book proved to be cover-to-cover model railroading inspiration, especially for anyone who knows and loves steam railroads and New Hampshire mountain scenery. While my 21st century ecological conscience deplores the depredations of these old-time clear-cut loggers, as a railroad buff and amateur historian, I'm fascinated by the determination and audacity of the larger-than-life 19th century logging barons. And the railroads they created are made for modeling: Here is everything you could want in a logging prototype, but on a far more manageable and modest scale than the megalithic operations of the big Pacific Northwest lumber companies.

The mill is all

The New Hampshire mountains of the 19th century were clad in virgin forests of spruce and Douglas fir, trees of good size and straight growth, ideal for lumber and boards of the highest quality. Rather then moving the felled timber too far, most of the White Mountain logging companies worked it in their own mills, some of which were considerable affairs.

The Swift River company's Conway board mill was for some time the largest in New England, with a capacity of several hundred thousand board-feet in a year. Most of them were smaller than this monster, but even the smallest was loading out enough finished lumber to keep the mainline railroad carriers busy (and happy). There was also a fair traffic in pulpwood for the newly emerging paper industry and in slabs and trimmings for fuel; nothing much got wasted.

Many of the railroads were centered on the mill, which divided them effectively into two halves: the pure rough-and-rugged logging lines—many of them temporary—extending into the hills upstream of the mill, and a better-laid and more easily graded railroad carrying finished lumber to the connection with the mainline carriers. Many of these connecting roads were worked by mainline locomotives and equipment.

The mills themselves were often built where two or three mountain side valleys came together, areas that typically provided a level site and had plenty of water for ponds, for driving machinery, or supplying boilers to work a steam plant. Around the mill grew up the short-lived townships of the logging era, some of them surprisingly large and well provided with stores, saloons, churches, and public buildings—not to mention the sort of disreputable establishment usually found in frontier settlements, which these effectively were.

Alongside the mill and the town lay the yard and facilities of the railroad, usually including an enginehouse of some sort with attached repair shop, water tank, coal stockpile (many of the logging engines were coal-fired to cut down on sparks and brands), spurs to hold the various items of special equipment, run-around loops, and sufficient yard tracks to marshal and hold the log trains and the carloads of finished lumber ready for dispatch.

This is all grist to the modeling mill, although to provide the structures, you'll be looking more to craftsman kits or a spot of scratchbuilding rather than searching the plastic kits on your dealer's shelves. But creating individual structures and detailed scenes is a lot of the appeal of modeling this kind of railroad. It's the opposite extreme to shake-the-box model railroading.

The track on the logging lines was light, but not always as light as you might think. Although the temporary lines and spurs might make do with 50-pound rail and a few twisted ties held in place with the odd shovelful of dirt, the main routes were laid in stouter stuff. Plenty of good-sized straight ties and 70- or even 80-pound rail was more the thing. The ballast might still be dirt and cinders, but there was plenty of it. The outbound tracks were often pretty much to the same standard as a regular Class 1 railroad, with a good weight of rail, a well-graded and drained alignment, and sometimes even proper stone ballast.

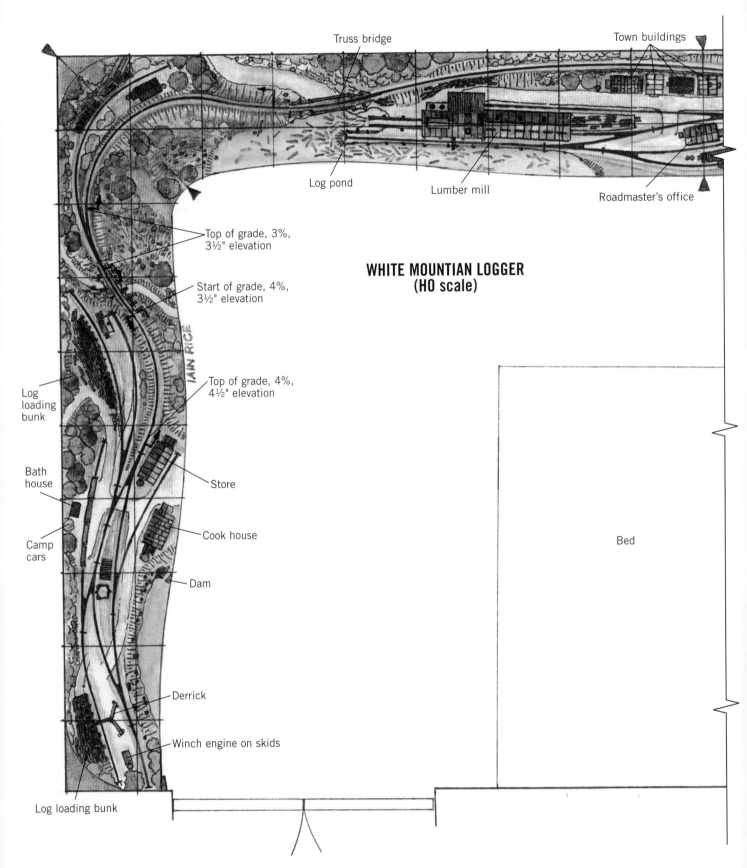

Truss bridge

Town buildings

Log pond

Lumber mill

Roadmaster's office

Top of grade, 3%,
3½" elevation

Start of grade, 4%,
3½" elevation

**WHITE MOUNTIAN LOGGER
(HO scale)**

IAN RICE

Top of grade, 4%,
4½" elevation

Log
loading
bunk

Bath
house

Store

Camp
cars

Cook house

Bed

Dam

Derrick

Winch engine on skids

Log loading bunk

In modeling terms, Micro-Engineering's code 70 and code 55 flextrack would work, although you'll need to look to Shinohara for a lot of the turnouts. The company's code 70 range has some useful short-number switches including a No. 4 in standard and wye versions. Walther's code 83 line also has useful wye switches, including a dinky No. 2½. Although it's OK for yard track and the logging main line, flextrack is a little too tidy for true backwoods logging iron. Here, a spot of hand-spiking works wonders—and if you're not too good at it, that will look just fine.

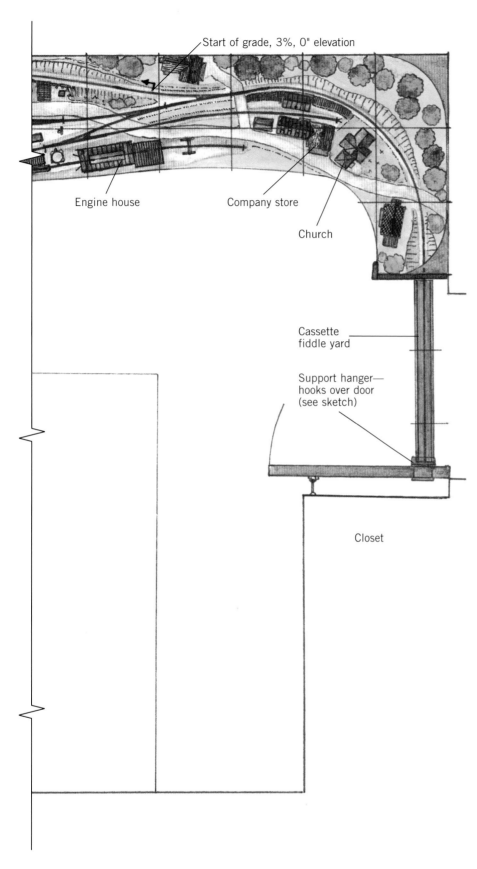

Start of grade, 3%, 0" elevation

Engine house

Company store

Church

Cassette
fiddle yard

Support hanger—
hooks over door
(see sketch)

Closet

Logging power

Logging in the White Mountains started in earnest in the 1870s and lasted up to the World War II period, but was at its height around the turn of the 20th century. As a historical modeling proposition, much will depend on finding the appropriate motive power.

Geared engines apart, the characteristic locomotives were a few of the chunky 0-4-0 tender switch engines built by the Portland company, together with a host of Baldwin's off-the-shelf 35-ton 2-4-2 saddle-tank industrial engines—a type which was built in the thousands for several gauges and powered mining, logging, and industrial railroads worldwide.

One of these logging Baldwins—the East Branch & Lincoln's No. 5—survives in working order on the White Mountain Central Museum railroad in Lincoln, N.H. The 35-ton Baldwin has appeared from time-to-time as a brass model, but as far as I'm aware, the Portland never has. Pity.

Other rod engines mentioned or illustrated in the book include a Porter 0-4-0T switch engine (not unlike the immortal Varney dockside model) and the ubiquitous Porter Mogul (2-6-0), which has long been available in brass in the iconic shape of the Ken Kidder kit (there's one listed on eBay as I write this). Taking a slightly more freelanced approach would suggest Mantua's 0-6-0T switcher as a starting point.

Geared steam is far more straightforward, with a good selection of Shays and a smattering of Climax and Heisler engines having been used. Most common were the Shays: two- and three-truck examples of various vintages and weights up to 90 tons.

Bachmann's 80-ton three-truck Shay is right on the mark for a White Mountain logging road set in the 1920s or later; the wood-cab version would be more typical. The old Roundhouse/ Model Die Casting kit Shay would also be a good basis to work on, and quite a few of those can be found second-hand for not much money. A bit more out-of-the-way are the older, smaller Shays. One of my favorites (if you like a bit of a challenge) is Keystone's long-running cast-metal kit for the diminutive 20-ton two-cylinder class A, for which North-West Short Line makes a drive-line kit. This would be perfect for a New England logger from about 1885 on; I've got one of these laid by for my own "someday" logging line.

The exquisite brass two-truck T-boiler Shay by PFM/United (Mich-Cal No. 2) is also still to be found at second-hand brass dealers—ideal for the pre-

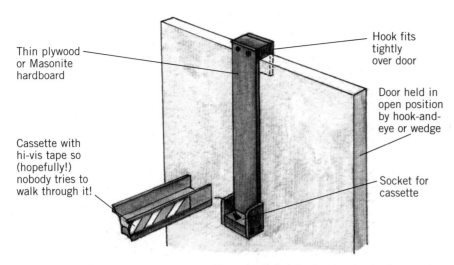

Thin plywood or Masonite hardboard

Cassette with hi-vis tape so (hopefully!) nobody tries to walk through it!

Hook fits tightly over door

Door held in open position by hook-and-eye or wedge

Socket for cassette

The end of the fiddle yard can be supported by a simple hanging bracket that hooks over the top of the door. This avoids having to permanently mount a bracket on the door.

1890 period on the smaller lines, but it won't be cheap. Other geared locomotive choices would include Bachmann's lovely two-truck 55-ton Class B Climax, good for 1900 and onward, and the Rivarossi two- and three-truck Heislers, more typical of the post-1920 era.

To go with these engines, you'll need connect and disconnect log bunks (made by Rivarossi, Kadee, Keystone, and Bachmann), stake-sided 36- and 40-foot flatcars, and 36-foot wooden gondolas with the ends knocked out. Stores and supplies arrived in older wood-side boxcars, often coming as far as the main yard behind Maine Central or Boston & Maine road power. At least one road—the Zealand—had a passenger car, an ancient wood-sided combine that looked to have first seen the light of day sometime around 1865. The old MDC/Roundhouse Virginia & Truckee cars would pass muster.

I haven't traced any pictures of cabooses, either the sort of shanty-on-wheels Kadee or Keystone make, or something more conventional. However, they're mentioned in written accounts, and as several of these logging lines operated trains over MeC and B&M track, they must have rostered some tail-end equipment. Four-wheel "bobbers" would be a fair bet.

Like logging roads elsewhere, the New Hampshire lines also possessed a fair selection of oddball and home-built equipment: tank cars for water or oil (not a regular tank car, mind; more like a flatcar with any kind of a tank lashed to it), firefighting cars carrying pumps and hose, pile-drivers, boom cars, flats to carry skidders, winches, and other machinery, and bunk and kitchen cars for use at temporary logging camps. You won't find much of this sort of thing out there ready-to-run, although there are a few useful kits and loads of gorgeous detail parts (from Keystone again). It pretty much comes down to adapting regular cars to fit the bill—which is, after all, what the full-size roads did.

The layout

This layout uses a 10 x 15-foot bedroom site, much the same size as Elm Point although with a different room configuration. This is the spare bedroom of a good-size bungalow, with French doors leading out to a terrace; ideal for bringing the baseboards in.

The design also features the ultimate in stripped-down bare-basics fiddle yards—a simple cassette spanning the room doorway. This presents another approach to the "what to do with the door" problem: fix it in the open position with a cabin hook when the layout is in use and hang the far end of the fiddle yard off it. Where cosmetic considerations rule out a cassette support fixed to the door, I use my removable "door-hanger," as in the sketch.

My plan, as usual, aims to capture the spirit of these lines in general rather than the specifics of any one prototype, and so draws together elements from several locations into a fictional-but-typical affair, which I've christened the Adams Branch & Tremont: Adams,

for New Hampshire's railfan governor Sherman Adams, and Tremont after the mountain of that name on the south side of the Saco valley. It inhabits the same general area as the Sawyer River RR, taking off west of the MeC's long grind up to Crawford and snaking up into the hills toward Mount Nancy.

The centerpiece of the layout, the mill and yard at Adams, are deemed to be situated on a high mountain flat a mile or two in from the junction with the Mountain Division, with the pure logging road continuing up into the hills beyond on a tortuous grade.

Adams is largely inspired by Livermore, on the real Sawyer River RR, home to the modest Mill No. 1 and the newer and larger Mill No. 2—after which my mill is patterned—as well as the SRRR's one-horse engine facility. Livermore itself was a surprisingly raffish little town strung out along a narrow defile, with the railroad climbing up behind it. I've made more of the engine facility and contented myself with only one mill, but otherwise Adams keeps pretty much to the spirit of the place.

Below the yard switch, the main line runs a little way behind elements of downtown Adams—including the all-important company store—before heading into a basic fiddle yard consisting of a cassette slung across the open doorway supported by the door hanger. Outbound trains would typically have been quite short, four to six cars of lumber running maybe twice a day, so there's no need for anything more sophisticated.

The log trains also have to run a little way along this track before they can clear the yard switch and setback to reach the unloading facility at the mill. Above Adams, the logging line proper climbs sharply at better than 3 percent along a hillside ledge, passing a typical log landing or intermediate loading point and crossing a trestle over a side creek before reaching Camp 12, based on the site of that name on the East Branch & Lincoln, with a big multi-tier log bunk and skidway, and a row of rail-mounted logger's bunkhouses. There's a crude log-loading derrick, a storehouse and, of course, the centerpiece of any logging camp—the cookhouse. Boiled mutton and beans, anyone?

CHAPTER NINE

Ice House Rock
(N scale)

The idea for this California-themed slice of big-time railroading springs—as have so many of the schemes I've dreamed up over recent years—from books that have come my way courtesy of Roger Meiner, the man mainly responsible for my education in matters of the U.S. prototype. There are two volumes at the root of this bit of "faction" based on mainline Southern Pacific operations in north-central California at the end of WWII: *Pacific Fruit Express,* by Anthony Thompson, Robert Church, and Bruce Jones (Central Valley RR Publications, 1992) and *Southern Pacific in the Bay Area,* by George Drury (Kalmbach Books, 1996).

Reefer train action may be the mainstay of this Southern Pacific layout, but the star is undoubtedly Train 51/52, The *San Joaquin Daylight.* Here GS-2 No. 4412 pulls out of Bakersfield, Calif., in August 1952. *Richard Steinheimer*

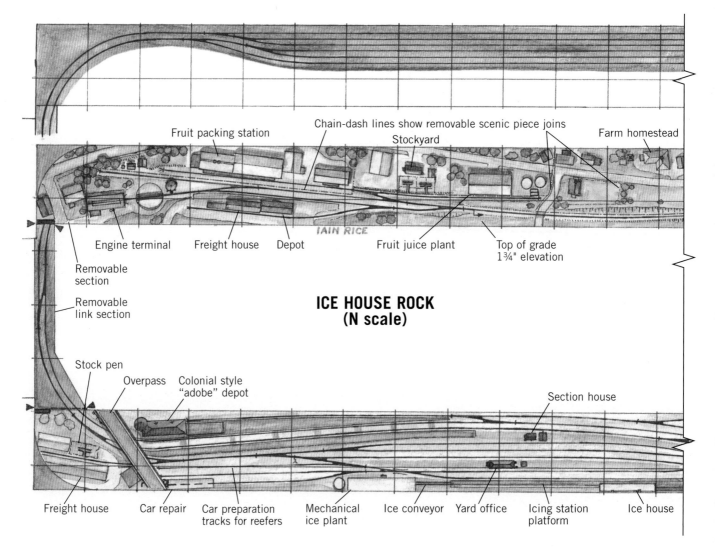

Fruit packing station

Chain-dash lines show removable scenic piece joins

Stockyard

Farm homestead

Engine terminal   Freight house   Depot   Fruit juice plant   Top of grade 1¾" elevation

Removable section

Removable link section

IAIN RICE

ICE HOUSE ROCK
(N scale)

Stock pen

Overpass   Colonial style "adobe" depot

Section house

Freight house   Car repair   Car preparation tracks for reefers   Mechanical ice plant   Ice conveyor   Yard office   Icing station platform   Ice house

From these sources come the twin themes around which this proposal is based: large-scale refrigerator car operations for the California fruit and produce trade and the ultra-glamorous passenger train operations of the SP north and south of its home base of San Francisco. We're talking lots of yellow reefers and gorgeous black, red, and orange *Daylight* passenger trains And yes, Kato's exquisite new N scale GS-4 steam locomotive and matching *Daylight* cars—just introduced as I set out to concoct this fruit express cocktail—did have something to do with it!

California themin'

California-themed layouts have long been popular among model railroaders—usually centered on the various routes through the Western mountain chains and across the Continental Divide. Famous locations such as Niles Canyon, the Cajon or Donner passes,

Tehachapi Loop, and Keddie Wye have figured countless times on western-themed layouts, while iconic big-time western motive power such as Union Pacific's Big Boy, Challenger, and FEF-4 Northern, SP's unique Cab-Forwards and GS-series Northerns, and Santa Fe's powerful 3800-series 2-10-2s and warbonnet-scheme diesels have long topped the best-seller lists of model motive power.

But there's another side to California railroading—a much gentler and more pastoral aspect that sees lazy branch lines serving the rolling groves of the mountain foothills or the fertile flatlands of the Central Valley. A tangled skein of through routes run north-south through the rich heart of the state, linking the sprawling vastness of Los Angeles in the south with the great conurbations of the Bay Area farther north, then stretching on to the Oregon border.

Probably the most glamorous of these north-south links is SP's coastal line through Santa José and Santa Barbara, route of the famed *Coast Daylight*. However, the real trunk of California railroading was the inland mileage of the Espee, Santa Fe, and, farther north, the Western Pacific.

In this case, it's Espee's San Joaquin Valley route that's my starting point, heading initially north then east out of Oakland through Antioch before looping southward to pass east of the Coast Range mountains down the wide San Joaquin valley to Merced, where it met the rival Santa Fe route. The two roads met again at Fresno, south of which there was a real tangle of alternate SP and ATSF routes, with branch lines firing off in all directions, before they converged again at Bakersville for the joint run to Mojave and the SP's northern approach to LA through Burbank, the junction with the Coast route.

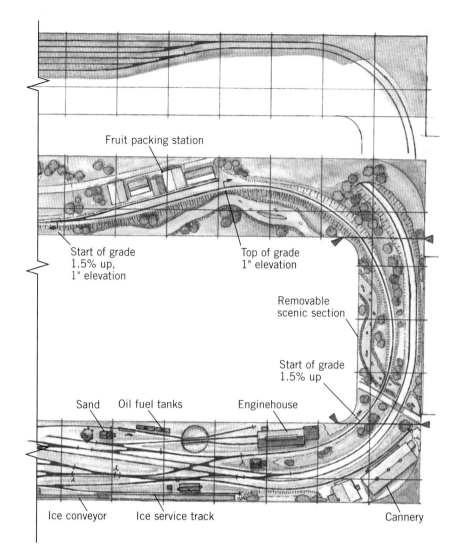

Fruit packing station

Start of grade
1.5% up,
1" elevation

Top of grade
1" elevation

Removable
scenic section

Start of grade
1.5% up

Sand   Oil fuel tanks   Enginehouse

Ice conveyor   Ice service track

Cannery

Factional railroading

I don't doubt there are any number of prototype locations amid this lot that would make a great starting point for a model railroad, but an awful lot of the trackage in the eastern Valley was Santa Fe, and for this scheme I was keen to fly Espee's flag. Also, many of the facilities for which I could locate prototype data were alarmingly large; things tend to sprawl somewhat in this part of the world! So I decided on a little "faction" by taking a real location on the railroad, but developing it in a fictional way. I set out with a combination of a 1948 Rand-McNally railroad atlas, a set of California state maps, and the incredible eye-in-the-sky capabilities of Google Earth to find a suitable location for a little tinkering with railroad history.

It was the northern section of the SP route, where the railroad raced across the wide, low-lying spaces of the San Joaquin valley through rich agricultural areas with the Sierra Nevada Mountains not far to the east, that struck me as offering the best potential for a believable and attractive "might have been" railroad. There were few branch lines in this neck of the woods and not many towns, so I had to get a bit creative. After a lot of deliberation and plotting on the ground courtesy

Hidden staging

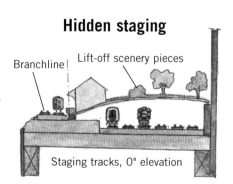

Branchline   Lift-off scenery pieces

Staging tracks, 0" elevation

This cross section of the branchline benchwork shows the concealed staging yard.

of Google, I decided to build myself a complete new town on the SP main line south of Merced, with a branch line taking off to the southwest. My town is christened Plainsburg after a local road. (Well, if there's a Plainsburg Road, presumably there's a Plainsburg for it to lead to—although Google has never heard of it.)

Ice houses and adobe depots

So the city of Plainsburg, Merced County, Calif., (elevation 168 feet, pop. 3,850) is a pure invention. It sits, say I, astride the SP's double-track San Joaquin Valley main and is the junction for the six-mile branch line to (equally fictional) East Grant, location of several major fruit-packing and canning enterprises.

Plainsburg features two California signatures: a Pacific Fruit Express reefer icing station and an arcaded Spanish-style depot, all red pantiles and white-plastered walls. It also has a small four-track classification yard clear of the main, serving the branch line to East Grant and that from Chowchilla (five miles farther south) to Dairyland (which did exist).

Adjacent to the yard are the tracks serving the icing facility and the refrigerator car yard. This last was where the cars were cleaned, serviced, and, if necessary, repaired or pre-cooled. Repairs are handled with a RIP (repair-in-place) track and small repair shop, one of many PFE "light-repair facilities." At the other end of the yard, a long freight house handles LCL ladings and non-perishable consignments, while a stockyard with loading ramps handles the livestock aspects of local farming.

Other spurs serve the ice house, produce storage warehouses, and several on-line industries including a box and crate works, two canneries, a farm equipment supplier, and a fuel depot. And, at the north end, handy for the junction, stands the modest engine terminal that caters to the needs of the small posse of 2-6-0s and 2-8-0s that run the branch lines and local road freights, plus the assigned switcher that looks after the yard and the icing station.

An icing crew skids 300-pound blocks into refrigerator-car bunkers at Coachella, Calif. Note the chain conveyor at left carrying the ice blocks along the platform. *Donald Sims*

Plainsburg is situated toward the eastern slopes of the San Joaquin valley, not far from the Sierra foothills, which would form an attractive backdrop to this narrow slice of fruit-and-farming country. The trackage is mostly straight; in this easy railroading country, there are many miles of tangent track and such curves as there are only change direction by a few degrees. By contrast, the mountain and coast sections of the Espee always look as if they were laid out with limp spaghetti. This section of the "Valley" line is a racing ground for the *San Joaquin Daylight,* which would blast through Plainsburg at 80-per with air-horn howling and headlights blazing. But the real business of this region is agriculture in all its aspects: cereals, beets, dairying, and livestock—plus the "top end" perishables: fruit and produce. And these are what underpins the enterprise that dominates these western rails: Pacific Fruit Express.

Pacific Fruit Express

The progenitor of the "Great Orange Fleet" was a child born of the Harriman empire, when the UP and SP were effectively under common management. PFE was formed in 1906 as a separate corporation jointly owned by the two railroads. It was set up to furnish the refrigerator cars and ice services required by the two owning railroads and their allies. The allies

mentioned were mostly the railroads further east—the Chicago & North Western, Rock Island, Illinois Central, New York Central, Erie, and Pennsylvania—that brought the California produce traffic across the Midwest through Chicago and on to the East. At various times, upstart Western Pacific was also granted ally status; the enemy, of course, was the Santa Fe and its rival Santa Fe Refrigerator Despatch operation.

By 1950, PFE's car fleet was simply enormous—some 38,500 cars, many built in PFE's own shops. They were intensively worked, and PFE maintained a wide range of facilities both throughout the Californian growing areas and at intervals across the Continental U.S. to Midwestern and Eastern markets.

It is the PFE facility at Plainsburg that dominates the yard and operating pattern and determines its most striking and characteristic structure: the 10-car 440-foot-long icing station and the attendant ice storage building. This is a pretty small example, at least by PFE standards, and it's inspired by the facility at Hood River, Ore.

Essential ice

The lynchpin of the whole PFE operation between its inception and the successful advent of mobile mechanical refrigeration in the mid-1950s was the traditional 40-foot refrigerator car,

cooled by up to 5,000 pounds of melting ice carried in ice-bunkers at each end.

Large rectangular blocks of ice were chopped and loaded through the car's four roof hatches, which also controlled ventilation and melt rates. The ice was topped off periodically throughout the typical 10- to 14-day journey from California field to Eastern-seaboard store by means of icing stations located at strategic points along the route.

The procurement, production, shipping, and storage of ice were a major preoccupation of PFE, and the icing stations at which the frozen blocks were whisked up to elevated platforms and manhandled into the car bunkers were the key facilities on which the whole operation depended.

Some of these ice transfer stations were huge, capable of servicing two 100-car consists simultaneously and with amazing rapidity. A good icing crew could fill a car's bunkers with as much as 3,600 pounds of the white stuff in little more than a minute. Four such crews could re-ice a 100-car train in well under an hour.

The ice came in 22 x 22-inch blocks of 10, 15, or 20-inch thickness, cut to fit through the 24 x 24-inch hatch openings; a 22 x 22 x 20-inch block weighed some 300 pounds. The blocks were moved up and along the icing platforms by special chain conveyors. From there the crews would skid them to the hatches using steel ice picks and wooden or steel ramps.

The biggest transfer stations were long enough to hold an entire 100-car consist (4,400 feet, or well over three-quarters of a mile) but most were shorter. The train would be moved as needed under "blue flag" rules (the train can't be moved when a blue flag was displayed, indicating men were working on train) or by special semaphore control, to bring the appropriate cuts of cars alongside the icing platform.

As well as the elevated platform serving the icing tracks, the transfer facility would need a source of ice—a warehouse where natural ice was brought in during the winter, or in later days, a plant where ice was made mechanically. In the early years of ice-reefer operation, the ice was harvested from natural sources such as mountain lakes that froze in winter. The ice was cut into blocks and stored in heavily-insulated ice houses until needed. Where the ice source was some distance from the point of use, the cut blocks were shipped to the ice house of the transfer station in insulated ice-service cars (which were often older reefers with the ice bunkers removed and extra insulation installed).

Block ice was used until ice-bunker reefers were phased out in the 1960s and early '70s. As PFE typically used around 1.6 million tons of ice a year, natural sources continued to be important and trains of ice service cars were a regular feature to the end.

Long thin site, buried staging

The long thin site for which this N scale slice of the ice action was conceived is probably the ultimate shelf layout natural. It's a passageway linking the front reception area of a house directly to a garden patio area. The passage is 20 feet long but only 6½ feet wide, with an outward-opening double French door on the garden end. The passageway itself had to remain clear and usable to a width of at least 3½ feet down the center, which meant that the railroad could only occupy a relatively narrow 18-inch strip down each side.

It's perfect for shelf format. With easily removable link pieces at each end to complete an oval, it presents a continuous-run footprint. Unusually for one of my designs, the front edges of the layout are dead straight and parallel to the walls—the practical considerations of the passageway function in this case taking precedence over my aesthetic scruples.

So this is a layout footprint occupying identical 18-inch-wide shelves running down either side of the passage. One scene consists entirely of Plainsburg yard, but the other is split to accommodate a hidden six-track ladder staging yard on the main line plus the branch line to East Grant.

The real business of the San Joaquin Valley route was perishable traffic headed east. Number 3509 is a hefty 2-8-4 that started life on the Boston & Maine. *Fred H. Matthews, Jr.*

A well-constructed set of hidden ladder staging using simple train detection to stop things in the right place should only need occasional access, so the entire staging area is buried beneath removable scenery pieces that enable the branch line scene to be a good visible depth.

As the topography of this region is no more than slightly rolling, the landscaping uses only gentle slopes and changes in elevation of a few feet. To get enough clearance to hide the staging beneath such landforms, the whole branchline scene is raised by means of a 1.5 percent grade, eventually reaching a height of 1¾ inches above the staging level at the approach to the terminus.

Scenic texture

Glue shell

Stiff metal mesh (old-fashioned wire porch screen is ideal)

Fixed scenery

Scenery profiles/bearers for lift-off pieces

The removeable scenery pieces are designed simply as standard glue-shell scenery sections built on a screen-wire base.

At East Grant, the staging turnout area lies beneath the easily removed buildings of the big packing station, and at the other end of the scene, a small packing facility and farm buildings perform the same function.

The remaining removable landscape pieces, which need only be about 8 inches wide, are intended to be ultra-lightweight and frameless, consisting simply of shaped sections of stiff metal screen-mesh covered in a thin layer of glue-shell surfacing and textured to match the fixed scenery. The sketch and cross-section on the plan should show how this works.

Trains

The star on this layout is, of course, the *San Joaquin Daylight*, trains 52 (southbound) and 51 (northbound)—a glorious ensemble in red, black, and orange behind a breathtaking GS-4. Con-Cor and Kato make the engine, and Kato most of the cars. For details of accurate consists, visit http://espee.railfan.net/san-joaquin.html.

Lesser mainline assignments might still rate a GS Northern or a 4-8-2 Mountain, but Pacifics are the general-purpose passenger power. Virtually all SP steam power, right down to the humblest switcher, trailed a distinctive Vanderbilt cylindrical-tank oil-bunker tender. Unfortunately, some otherwise-suitable model locomotives lack this vital appendage—

One of Southern Pacific's big Cab-Forwards leads a long string of ice-bunker refrigerator cars. *David P. Morgan Library collection*

although a bit of "ready-to-run mingling" can overcome this, as suggested for the 2-8-0s below. That said, there's enough Vanderbilt-equipped power out there to form a good foundation for this layout proposal.

Local passenger assignments typically rated older and smaller 4-6-2s, for which role Model Power's USRA light Pacific with Vanderbilt tender will certainly pass muster, trailing a short consist of plain heavyweight cars. Road freights would roll behind power ranging from a 2-8-0 or 2-8-2 through Mountains and Northerns to AC-class 4-8-8-2 Cab-Forwards. Model Power lists its USRA light Mikado in an SP version with the correct round-tank tender, and Con-Cor has the heavy version, also with the proper tender.

Likewise, Bachmann's husky 4-8-4 Northern comes in a convincing Vanderbilt/SP version. The company's 4-8-2 USRA light Mountain is listed in SP paint but with a normal coal tender, which robs it of the SP look. The same goes for Con-Cor's USRA 2-10-2.

Anyway, SP favored 4-10-2s for drag freights. The heaviest hotshots—long strings of PFE reefers—rolled behind Mountains or Northerns on the plains, while Cab-Forwards performed the service through the mountains.

At the other end of the motive power scale, the backbone of the branch line workings were the many small 2-6-0 and 2-8-0 engines that SP had left over from an earlier era. Model Power has an SP 2-6-0 with Vanderbilt tender that's right on the money, while Bachmann's generic Consolidation will pass muster if you equip it with a Model Power Vanderbilt tender.

If you can't obtain the tender as a spare, then just buy a couple of extra Vanderbilt-fitted USRA Pacific or 2-8-2 engines and swap the tenders for the USRA type that comes with the Bachmann 2-8-0. Sell the surplus engines on eBay and you've got yourself some authentic-looking SP branchline power for only a few dollars extra!

The same dodge will get you an SP-looking switcher, mating the Model

Power tender from the 2-6-0 with a Bachmann 0-6-0 USRA switch engine, although in that case, I'm not sure what you'd do with a 2-6-0 with a slope-back tender!

Diesel power is simply not a problem. Virtually every diesel type SP owned at this time is available in SP paint, notably the charismatic black widow freight scheme. For instance, Atlas offers its characterful Baldwin V1000 in SP black-and-orange—an ideal alternate switch engine for the Plainsburg yard. Both heavyweight and smooth-side passenger equipment is also widely offered—although I fancy quite a lot of what is listed in *Daylight* paint is flying false colors.

There's also a wide choice of PFE reefers covering most of the distinctive car classes that made up the PFE fleet. A comprehensive listing of authentic SP equipment in N scale can be found at Pete McClosky's invaluable Southern Pacific Web Resources page at http://www.sphts.org/pmcclosky/spwebresources.html.

CHAPTER TEN

Downtown approach
(N scale)

Chicago, in railroad terms, is the jungle. Even today, as your train heads in to Union Station, it threads a maze of junctions, yards, and seemingly inexplicable multi-track sections, crossing other multi-track lines at multi-diamond junctions and passing under bridges carrying still more railroads going who-knows-where. And this is now; not so long ago things were even more complex.

The Chicago skyline looms above a Chicago & North Western freight train rolling past the Erie Street coach yard. *C&NW*

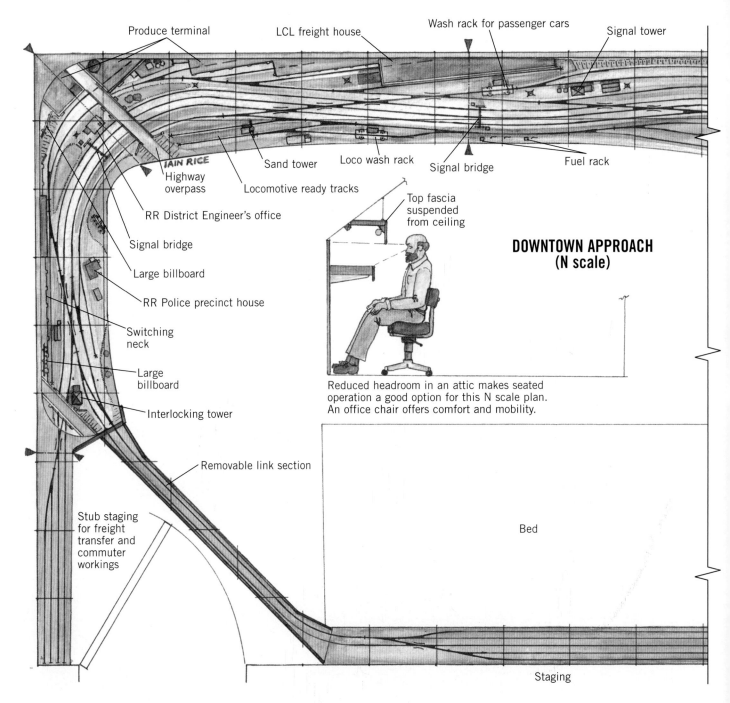

Produce terminal

LCL freight house

Wash rack for passenger cars

Signal tower

IAIN RICE

Highway overpass

Sand tower

Loco wash rack

Signal bridge

Fuel rack

Locomotive ready tracks

RR District Engineer's office

Signal bridge

Large billboard

RR Police precinct house

Switching neck

Large billboard

Interlocking tower

Removable link section

Stub staging for freight transfer and commuter workings

Top fascia suspended from ceiling

DOWNTOWN APPROACH
(N scale)

Reduced headroom in an attic makes seated operation a good option for this N scale plan. An office chair offers comfort and mobility.

Bed

Staging

The abandoned facilities you see on every hand from the Superliner window would have been active, trains would have threaded the many rights-of-way now trackless and weed-grown, and even the still-active trackage over which you're riding would have seen a lot more action.

To me, the approaches to major terminals or union stations, with their complex junctions, multiple tracks, car yards, engine terminals, freight houses and mail/express facilities, all crammed between towering city buildings and laced with a surprising number of industry tracks, are far more interesting than the actual stations themselves.

And they're far more modelgenic, not to mention rich in interesting operational potential.

When you're pushed for space or modeling time, then concentrating on the most-interesting aspects of a subject and placing the rest off-scene has always struck me as a good idea. It's another form of "bitsa" modeling (see Chapter 3)—using a modest site to represent just a part of a large subject rather than going the more conventional route of modeling a smaller subject in its entirety.

In this case, I'm choosing to model the station approach but not the station

itself, the only part of which to feature being the extreme outbound ends of the platform tracks, where the power sits idling.

In fact, modeling the approach rather than the actual station commends itself for a number of reasons, chiefly that it addresses one of my personal frustrations with model railroading. It's an anomaly I call the "pillar of salt syndrome," which is the contrast between our trains moving beautifully realistically while everything else is frozen solid. And nowhere do I find this lack of animation in the general environment more jarring than when

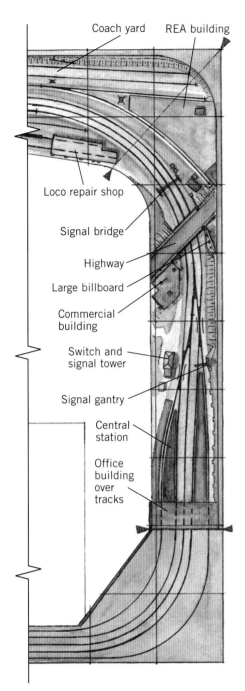

Coach yard
REA building
Loco repair shop
Signal bridge
Highway
Large billboard
Commercial building
Switch and signal tower
Signal gantry
Central station
Office building over tracks

modeling a scene—like the platforms of a major railroad station or a busy downtown street—that would in reality be bustling with life and movement.

As much as I admire the brilliant cityscapes I see in the pages of *Model Railroader*, which certainly look great in photos, I couldn't live with all that suspended animation.

However, modeling just the railroad environs as it threads the downtown area of a big city neatly gets you out of this conundrum, as the right-of-way typically runs behind and beneath the city's structures, hidden away from highways, malls and plazas behind high

fencing and walls, advertising signs, and strip-built structures teetering along the railroad margins. It's almost a secret world, away from the bustling citizenry and having a life of its own.

The city train environment is given over 100 percent to railroading. Not many folks will be found wandering around these parts. Mostly, what moves are the trains—lots of them, ranging from a transcontinental threading its way in from the West Coast to local switch and transfer moves and light engines making their way to servicing facilities. And that's animation we can model convincingly.

And then there are the facilities themselves: engine terminals, car yards, wash racks, repair sheds, mail and express warehouses, LCL freight houses, classification yards, cold-storage complexes, industries of all sorts, maintenance-of-way depots, spare equipment storage spurs—all made for modeling. These give scope for operating a lot of equipment in a small space, for such downtown facilities, often squeezed in on tight, odd-shaped sites, are intensively used and usually crowded with cars.

There's almost no piece of railroad equipment you couldn't plausibly place in such a scene, from a multi-unit lash-up of sleek express diesels to a rusty Jordan spreader.

Downtown on the shelf

The sort of compact long and narrow site offered by a shelf layout format is ideally suited to modeling downtown railroading.

Out in the wide-open spaces, railroad facilities can sprawl over thousands of acres, but in the heart of a city they're hemmed in at every hand, squeezed and confined by big buildings and tight city blocks. It's rare for railroads in these locations to take up much width. Often, the facilities are strung out along the main lines in a sort of ribbon of convoluted sidetracks.

If pure railroading is your primary interest, then a layout like this is ideal as the non-railroad scenery consists of little more than a few building flats, retaining walls, fences, and advertising signs along the rear of the scene.

In this case I have added a handful of foreground structures to act as view-blocks to increase the visual interest and to break up the long, thin look somewhat, creating a series of smaller scenes within the context of the whole.

This is just the sort of model railroad for which N scale is made. Sure, you could do something similar in HO, but not on a handy shelf around the walls of a small (9 x 13-foot) townhouse attic and still have it function as a guest or student bedroom.

Attic rooms like this have advantages and problems as sites for shelf layouts. On the plus side, natural lighting by skylights means there's no window to take up a good portion of one wall. Working against that are the sloping ceiling and low eave along one side of the room that restrict the mounting height for the layout.

Here, the compact cross-section of my suggested shelf presentation, with its close-coupled top fascia and 10-inch viewing gap helps. The low eave in this room is a little over four feet, which allowed a track height of 40 inches with a nine-inch high backdrop.

Coincidentally, this display height matched the conditions in my own attic railroad room, although for my larger scale layout I'm using a 12-inch backdrop. But the point is that with seated operation using an ordinary roll-around office chair, your eye level will typically be about 45 to 50 inches, right in the slot for a natural view of the model, with the horizon-line falling nicely within the height of the back-drop. You can fine-tune this simply by adjusting the seat height of the chair.

Although representing the approach to a terminal station, the layout is actually arranged as a continuous-run oval with double-ended ladder staging and a fiddle yard along one wall, in this case, tightly located on an eight-inch-wide shelf running above one side of the bed.

This off-stage facility serves to represent both the station itself and to act as rest-of-the-railroad staging for trains leaving the outbound end of the approach complex on the main line.

A further small set of stub-end staging tucked away behind the room door

A sea of refrigerator cars await unloading at the Chicago & North Western's Wood Street Yard in Chicago. The yard's many pairs of team tracks allowed trucks to back up directly to the reefers for unloading. *C&NW*

handles commuter trains and freight transfer runs. The two sets of staging connect at the junction at the outbound end of the scene. All mainline train movements originate and terminate in through staging, although you can certainly let trains just roll right around the oval in a display mode.

Normally, however, operation centers around trains arriving and departing the station, plus everything that happens in between in terms of train servicing and re-marshaling, motive power movements, and handling head-end business.

Of course, local switching and transfer runs move between the various facilities, freight movements to the LCL warehouse and industry tracks, and the workings needed to keep the various facilities stocked with essentials like fuel, sand, chemicals, foodstuff, and all the myriad supplies needed to replenish a long-distance passenger train.

Authentic flavor
I'm not going to pretend that my plan is based on any real locale. Rather, it dips freely into the full pot of Chicago prototype and signature elements to create a dish that has an authentic Chicago flavor.

So there are plenty of tracks—connected by ladders of double-slip

switches, spanned by color-light signal bridges, and controlled by close-spaced signal towers. The three-track main, snaking between buildings and diving beneath city streets, has inbound and outbound tracks sandwiching a bidirectional siding.

Facilities include a perishable-produce cold storage complex, three freight houses including a seriously long LCL terminal, a two-track coach-servicing yard with wash rack, an extensive Railway Express Agency depot, and an engine terminal with repair shed and a second wash rack.

The station, tucked away "in the basement" of a big building (in this case, the railroad's offices), is patterned after Chicago's old Central Station, erected by Illinois Central in 1893. It has four platform tracks and a central passing/escape track.

Other prototype elements borrowed or pecked at include a nod to the 40th Street coach yard, the Chicago Produce Terminal, IC's rather down-at-the-heels 21st Street engine terminal, and the long ex-Erie RR LCL freight house on the approach to Dearborn.

Less specifically but just as typically there are lots of big billboards facing trackside, areas of grass-and-weed no man's land between the tracks, and a myriad of small structures, including the duty engineer's office and a railroad

police squad house, all dotted around the railroad property.

All these ingredients were harvested from among the many photos of Chicago-area railroading featured in books and magazines. Many of the precise locations are, unfortunately, not identified in the captions, but there's certainly no shortage of prototype inspiration when it comes to the Windy City.

Track
Approaches to downtown stations like this are characterized by complex trackwork, of which the signature item is undoubtedly the double-slip or compound switch.

Peco offers these for N scale in its fine-looking code 55 Streamline series, together with single-slip compounds, matching diamonds, straight, wye and curved turnouts, and a double-scissors crossover. All these pieces are available in the all-live Electrofrog format, which provides continuous power to turnout frogs for the best slow running.

Used with matching code 55 flex-track, the Peco track enables you to represent just about any prototype arrangement, the only missing link being the rare three-way turnout. My design here does without that, but uses several double-slips. However, this Peco code 55 track does have a quirk,

Two Illinois Central passenger trains—The *Governor's Special* at left and the *City of New Orleans* at right—prepare to depart Central Station in Chicago on the IC's last day of passenger operations in April 1971. *B.L. Bulgrin*

in that all the turnouts no matter what radius or turnout length use the same frog angle of 10 degrees, equivalent to a nominal No. 6, as do the matching diamonds and slips.

What varies is the lead and hence the sharpness of the divergence from the straight, as described in my introductory notes to this section on page 39. In the context of this plan, all the turnouts are wide radius for the main running lines and medium for yard tracks.

This Peco code 55 track will handle any N scale equipment using the fine-looking low-profile wheelsets that are now pretty much standard. Rolling stock having clunky early standard deep-flange profiles can readily be modified by changing out the wheelsets for low-profile replacements.

I always think it's worth paying the extra for metal wheels from the likes of InterMountain or Kato, but Atlas or Micro-Trains molded nylon wheels work just fine. Freight or passenger cars can also be upgraded by fitting complete trucks from Kato, Atlas, Inter-Mountain, or Micro-Trains. For the latter, specify low-profile wheels. These trucks come complete with working knuckle couplers, which are much more realistic and offer more-versatile operation than the traditional N scale Rapido coupler.

To control complex track layouts like this one, tower-style interlocking panels would be the way to go. I recommend using Peco's clip-on under-the-turnout solenoid switch machines fired by Circuitron's No. 911202 momentary-contact panel-mount switches. A layout like this is a natural for DCC, but you'll need plenty of power districts to make fault-finding simple.

Working color-light signals would be a great addition, both visually and operationally. There's something very satisfying about having your engineers thread their trains through a complex interlocking solely under the guidance of the signals, with the train-driving and routing/controlling aspects of operation prototypically separated.

Trains galore

So much for the bread-and-butter; now for the cream-cake—the trains. With a 1960s-era generic Chicago setting the world is pretty much your oyster, with all the big names resident in town and a whole host of lesser roads that were soon to be fallen flags to choose. You have Rock Island, Chicago Great Western, Wabash, Erie, Illinois Central, Monon, Nickel Plate Road, and Gulf, Mobile & Ohio. And that's before you get to local efforts like the Indiana Harbor Belt, Elgin, Joliet & Eastern, or the Chicago Short Line. Mind

you, these were basically freight-hauling lines that didn't figure too much downtown.

Just about the only thing you wouldn't see in these surroundings would be a manifest freight or long unit trains of coal, grain, chemicals, or ore. Those ran on dedicated belt lines much farther out, linking the great freight yards like Proviso and the big industrial centers like South Bend or Gary. Downtown mostly belonged to passenger business—long distance and commuter—and the mail and express traffic associated with it.

Still, with a mix to choose from that includes EMD E units, Alco PAs, and classic covered wagons in a dozen paint schemes, first and second-generation hood units of every description (many boiler-equipped and in passenger service), a smattering of switchers, you'll see almost any kind of motive power.

Add to that the richly painted smooth-side and heavyweight steel passenger equipment, fluted-side stainless-steel cars, head-end cars of every kind, express boxcars, Flexi-Van containers, early Road-Railers, plus a wide range of freight cars for perishable, LCL, and railroad supply traffic, and I don't think there's any lack of scope or variety.

This is, after all, the Railroad Capital of America …

CHAPTER ELEVEN

Blue Hills and yonder
(On30 scale)

An East Tennessee & Western North Carolina (Tweetsie) narrow-gauge passenger train has just entered the dual-gauge track near Elizabethton, Tenn., in November 1943. *A.C. Hudson*

I can't deny I have an incurable soft spot for quaint back-home, back-then short lines featuring ancient steam-kettles, mixed trains, and wheel-high weeds. And where space, time, and money are in short supply, these can make ideal subjects for model railroads. Like the real thing, a model short line can get by on not much of anything—especially if it's narrow gauge. As a theme for a shelf layout, narrow gauge railroads are hard to beat. Shelves are, by and large, narrow—and so are slim-gauge railroads. That's pretty much the whole point of the things.

Narrow gauge modeling used to be something of a backwater of the model railroad hobby. Such models as there were in the popular sizes—HOn3, Sn3, and On3—were usually either costly in ready-to-run brass or came as craftsman kits for the skilled. But in recent years that changed with Bachmann's Spectrum line of high-quality RTR On30 equipment. Now O scale narrow gauge is as accessible as straight HO, for much the same order of cost and requiring similar elbow room.

Peco and Micro-Engineering now make dedicated On30 track, and there are plenty of fine O scale structure kits, figures, details, and accessories available, all just as suited to narrow gauge as standard gauge railroading.

On30 basically features O scale equipment operating on the standard HO 16.5mm track gauge, which in O scale equates to a track width of a tad over 30 inches—hence the designation of On30. Although 2' 6" is actually a very rare gauge at full size, visually it's not so different from the three-foot gauge used by the majority of America's narrow gauge railroads. The error between On30 and true On3 is only 2.5mm in the track gauge; no big deal. So most On30 equipment follows three-foot gauge prototypes and looks just fine. It's a size that has become deservedly popular, and there's now enough choice of locomotives and rolling stock to allow a range of prototype themes to be explored.

America's narrow gauge lines

With the notable exception of the group of railroads in Maine that operated on the ultra-slim two-foot gauge, common-carrier narrow gauge in America ran on rails a yard apart—as did the majority of private logging, mining or industrial lines. (Common-carrier railroads were those offering a public passenger and freight service and handling mail and express. Private railroads carried only the traffic of their owners.)

Narrow gauge railroads were normally built where difficult terrain or sparse traffic would have made a full-sized standard gauge road uneconomic. They required far less real estate and

got by with minimal roadbed, tighter cuts, and small-bore tunnels. They could follow a tightly curved alignment and climb steep grades, while the smaller and lighter equipment made bridge-building easier. Above all, narrow gauge railroads were cheap, and economics mattered when opening up poor country or linking together scattered communities in rugged mountain areas.

While odd little narrow gauge lines popped up all over the U.S. from 1875 to 1900, many of them were short-lived. Either they soon became inadequate and were rebuilt as standard gauge lines, or they became redundant and were swiftly torn up. Only in a few particular areas did narrow gauge lines stay and grow as a permanent feature of the railroad map.

Best-known of these grown-up narrow gauge systems was the extensive group of lines threading the mountains of Colorado, Nevada, and New Mexico. The Denver & Rio Grande, Rio Grande Southern, and Colorado & Southern among them operated hundreds of miles of slim-gauge track, often in spectacular mountain scenery, carrying ore, coal, precious metals, merchandise, and livestock. These railroads have long been a popular modeling subject and their better-known features, such as the famous Ophir Loop, have probably been modeled as often as such icons as Horseshoe Curve or Tehachapi Loop.

Less well-known were the three-foot gauge lines farther west. The mighty Southern Pacific had a surprisingly extensive network, the Carson & Colorado, running in eastern California and Nevada, but never quite got to Colorado. In California itself was another large system, the North Pacific Coast, together with several local railways like the delectable short line up to Lake Tahoe. Farther east, the Black Hills region of North Dakota was home to an amazing tangle of narrow gauge railways—mining, logging, and common-carrier.

I've based some of my previous narrow gauge layout proposals on Black Hills prototypes. Back in the East, three-foot gauge is much more rare,

with just two systems of note: the East Broad Top in Pennsylvania and the West Tennessee & Eastern North Carolina, or Tweetsie, which went pretty much where its name said it did.

Both these lines were coal-haulers, but there the resemblance ends. The EBT was big-time Appalachian coal railroading squeezed down to fit three-foot-wide tracks. It was all steel hoppers and eight-coupled steam locomotives. On the other hand, the Tweetsie's vintage Ten-Wheelers rambled amid the farmlands and squeezed into the steep southern hills pulling a few sway-backed wooden gondolas of coal mixed with the cows and the corn, along with the folks tagging along in back riding a snug combination car warm with a coal stove.

Slim-gauge short line

Forget the gauge for a minute: The Tweetsie was in every respect a classic back-country short line. In fact, part of it was mixed three-foot and standard gauge and quite busy and businesslike, but it was the purely slim-gauge Linnville River portion that took off into the scenic hill country and became, in its day, a railroad institution famous throughout the land.

"Mixed Train Daily" describes the Tweetsie's Linnville line perfectly. It had a verdant right of way that wound into beautiful blue-ridge hill country through picturesque farmland, past some of the oldest habitations in the whole U.S. It had quaint depots, with spurs that ran so far into the weeds that the cars looked as if they'd taken root. It crossed creeks on creaking iron truss bridges and teetered over a trestle or two. It reeled around horseshoe curves and squeezed through the steep-sided Doe River gorge. If you set out to imagine the most-characterful, most-appealing and most-modelable kind of short line railroad, you'd probably come up with the Tweetsie.

I'm glad to say that a part of the railroad lives to tweet another day in the form of the Tweetsie Railroad Park at Blowing Rock, N.C., one of the oldest railroad-themed attractions in the country. Although this three-mile loop of three-foot track doesn't use the original Tweetsie right of way, it does have the real McCoy for equipment in the shape of Baldwin 4-6-0 No. 12 and some cars, plus a lot of miscellaneous hardware. Tragically, many small Tweetsie and other local historical artefacts were lost when fire destroyed the railroad's restored depot-museum and gift shop in March 2008.

Right now, there's a bit of a stumbling-block when it comes to practical, authentic Tweetsie modeling in On30: no engines. Bachmann does make a fine model of the charismatic little Baldwin Ten-Wheeler, but only in its G scale range—a little large for indoor shelf-based railroads. That said, the smart money says it's got to be a strong contender for the On30 range soon. The Ten-Wheeler is the real missing link, and the Baldwin is the ideal pro-

totype. But that's then and this is now: What's out there to facilitate the creation of a model based on a similar— but freelance—slim-gauge prototype?

There's enough. Bachmann already lists two delightful small narrow gauge engines that fit the bill nicely: the dinky 2-6-0 Mogul and a charismatic 4-4-0. Both of these are available in an "Eastern" straight-stacked coal-burning version that would suit a Tweetsie-style layout, well—to a "T."

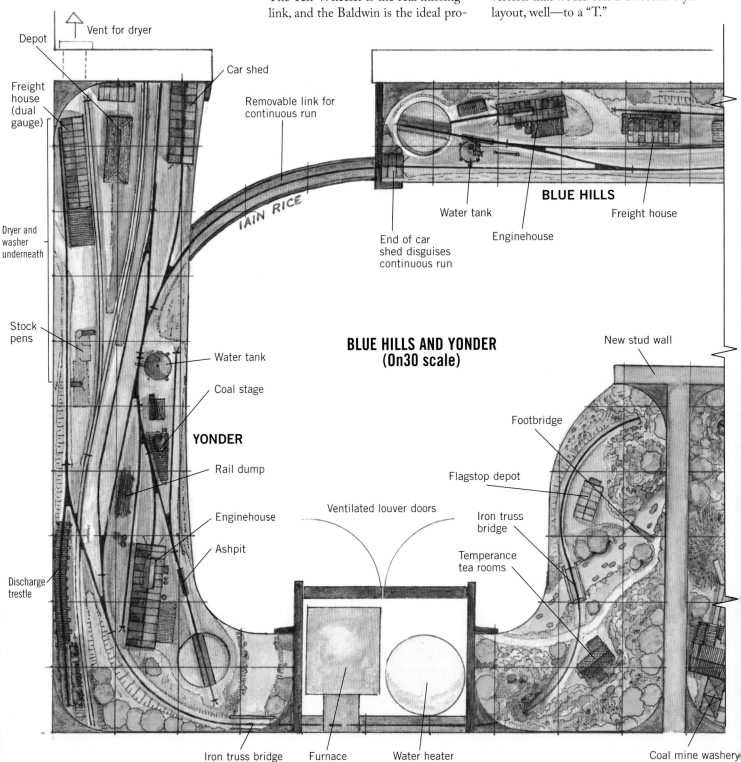

Depot

Vent for dryer

Car shed

Freight house (dual gauge)

Removable link for continuous run

IAIN RICE

Dryer and washer underneath

BLUE HILLS

Water tank

Enginehouse

Freight house

End of car shed disguises continuous run

Stock pens

Water tank

BLUE HILLS AND YONDER (On30 scale)

New stud wall

Coal stage

Footbridge

YONDER

Flagstop depot

Rail dump

Iron truss bridge

Enginehouse

Ventilated louver doors

Temperance tea rooms

Ashpit

Discharge trestle

Iron truss bridge

Furnace

Water heater

Coal mine washery and loader

A return to old haunts?

In the notes describing the Virginia and Truckee-based plan in my last Kalmbach layout design book (*Mid-Sized & Manageable Track Plans*), I confessed to an early attempt at U.S.-style model railroading allegedly set in the Blue Ridge mountains. The whole thing came about through ignorant schoolboy Rice confusing Virginia City, Colo., with Virginia the state—a geographical mish-mash that resulted in some of the world's more improbable model railroad scenery. Almost everything about this layout is best forgotten, except its name: the Blue Hills and Yonder. That seems to chime in nicely with the sort of theme I'm setting out to explore here.

So what we have is an end-to-end "route" layout depicting a true backcountry short line on the western side of the Blue Ridge. The BH&Y runs from an interchange with the standard gauge (Southern or Louisville & Nashville) at Yonder, where the yard features a shared freight house and stock pen and a ramped high-level track to allow coal to be transferred between narrow- and standard-gauge cars. The depot also serves both the standard and narrow gauges, although to ease the track-laying, only the narrow tracks are live.

For the same reason, I've resisted the temptation to indulge in any mixed gauge; it would be easy enough to introduce if you're happy to spike your own iron. There is a crossing between the standard and narrow gauges, but as the standard gauge is dummy this could be plain track "fudged" cosmetically.

Opposite the depot, the last few feet of a car-shed built to shelter the BH&Y's passenger equipment serves as a viewblock to disguise the point where the standard gauge meets the wall. A single-track enginehouse, turntable, and water tank make up the locomotive facilities.

After threading the badlands behind the basement furnace and water heater (chastely concealed by appropriate cabinetry), the line passes through a separate, self-contained scene inspired by the Doe Gorge section of the Linnville Branch, complete with tiny flag-stop depot and a refined Temperance Tea Room for the use of trippers to this scenic attraction.

The gorge takes up one side of the peninsula allowed by the T-shaped wall on the other side of which is the mine, really just a small coal tipple and washery with its associated dump. The line then runs into the intermediate passing place at Halfway (which it isn't), where there's also a spur serving a seed merchant and stock pen.

A last jog past a whiskey distillery brings the panting train to the terminus at Blue Hills, Tenn., passing a small feed mill and crossing main street before reaching the depot. There's another one-road engine house here; normally, one locomotive lives at each end of the line. Any third, spare engine would slumber at the rear of the Yonder enginehouse, which is just long enough to house two engines.

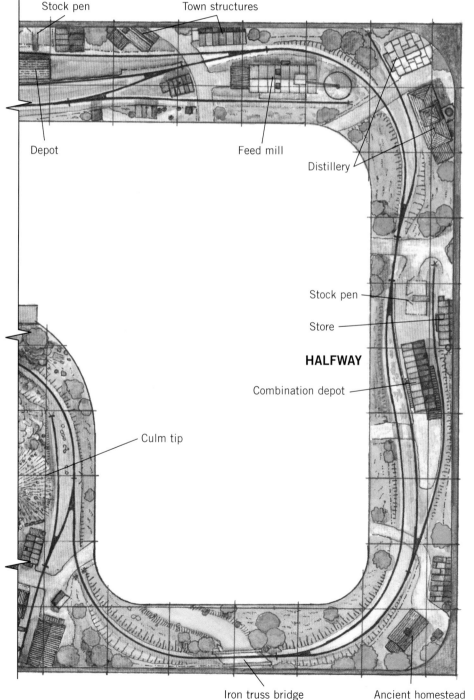

Stock pen
Town structures
Depot
Feed mill
Distillery
Stock pen
Store
HALFWAY
Combination depot
Culm tip
Iron truss bridge
Ancient homestead

The Tweetsie's daily mixed train heads out of Junction City, headed for Boone, N.C., in September 1936. Mixed trains were staples of both narrow- and standard-gauge shortlines. *Colorado Railroad Museum Collection*

Living with the laundry

The BH&Y is tucked into a small (roughly 10 x 18-foot) basement utility area in a modern townhouse—a site shared with the usual furnace and hot-water tank, laundry equipment and domestic storage. The laundry area is located at one end, close to the foot of the basement stairs, with the washer and dryer (front-loading) beneath the wide shelf carrying Yonder. The dryer vents into a duct into the garage area that occupies the rest of the basement.

To increase the available length of run and the amount of shelving above and below the railroad, the space is divided by a short stud wall that forms the basis of the double-scene peninsula. This has the effect of creating two completely separate viewing areas, which is a good way of increasing the apparent size of the layout.

The BH&Y occupies shelves of varying width, set around 50 inches above the floor. About half of the layout—the "wide" scenes of Yonder, Doe, Gorge and the mine—sits on gallows brackets fastened direct to the basement and stud walls. Situated above the laundry, the shelves are slightly more than two feet wide most of the way, a

tad more at each end. Where it sneaks behind the furnace and water heater, though, the line runs on a three-inch wide plank. This broadens back out to a little under two feet for the gorge and mine scenes, supported off the stud wall, which is T-shaped in plan to give a blind end to the peninsula.

In addition to adding useful support to the wide shelves, having this blind end discourages spectators from standing right where they're most in the way. Due to the overhead ducts from the furnace, there is no storage shelving above the layout over these wider scenes. The rest of the railroad, however, sits on track-supported shelves 18 inches or less in width with storage shelves above and beneath the model. The cabinetry that hides the furnace and water tank would need careful design and construction to meet building-code requirements for fire prevention and furnace air supply.

As is often the case when mixing model railroads with domestic needs, adequate and unobstructed access is essential. Model railroaders may be happy threading tight aisles, but family members carrying boxes for storage, laundry baskets, and the like won't be

wanting to hula their way through squeeze points. So the footprint of the layout has been tailored to give plenty of unobstructed floor space.

That this easy access suits the walkaround operation envisaged for the layout (using wireless DCC throttles but local fascia-mounted control of turnouts) is of course entirely coincidental.

The railroad itself is a dual-mode design in that it can be configured for two styles of operation. Basically, it's a pure old-fashioned end-to-end affair with trains shuttling between two terminal points, with an intermediate passing siding and industry.

Install the removable link section across the doorway, however, and you've got an oval continuous-run footprint for those occasions when you just want to let the trains trundle around while you relax—even if they do take a somewhat-improbable dive through the car-shed at Blue Hills!

Whatever mode the layout is operated in, the ruling curves are 21" radius, and most of the turnouts are Micro-Engineering No. 5s, with a few Peco wyes. Either ME or Peco flex-track would serve.

CHAPTER TWELVE

The EK sub
(N scale)

Appalachian coal-hauling has long been a popular theme for model railroading, as it offers a tempting mix of intensive operation with interesting structures and spectacular scenery. Most of the Appalachian layouts I've come across over the years have favored the big-time operations along the spine and down the eastern side of the mountains—essentially the hinterland of the great coal ports of the eastern seaboard and the coal catchment of the heart of heavy northeast industry around Pittsburgh.

A General Electric U30C leads an Alco and another GE at the head of a unit coal train near Mannington, Ky., in March 1979. *Jerry Mart*

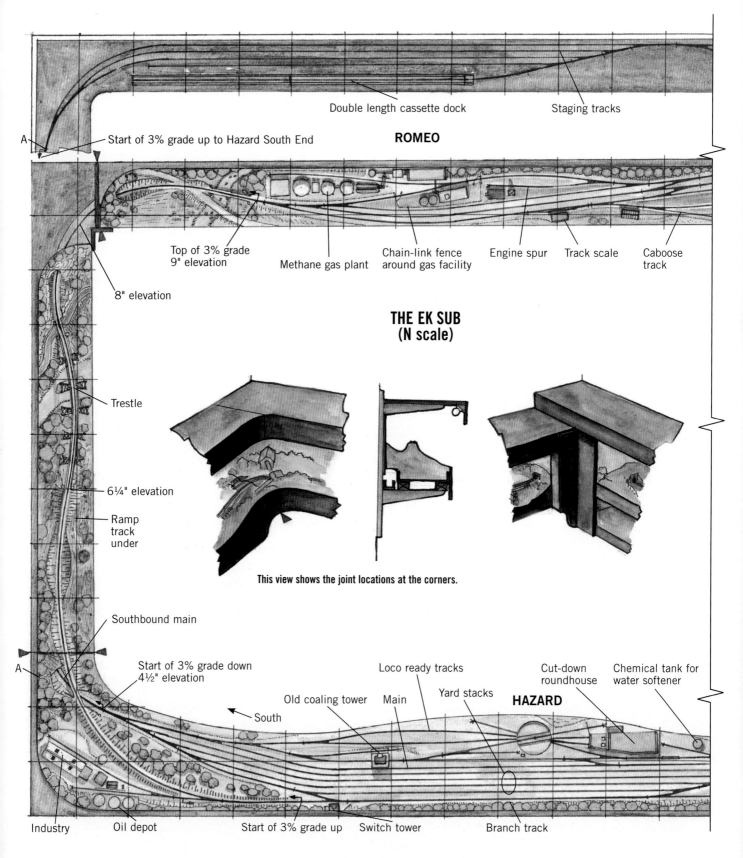

Double length cassette dock

Staging tracks

ROMEO

A

Start of 3% grade up to Hazard South End

Top of 3% grade
9" elevation

Methane gas plant

Chain-link fence
around gas facility

Engine spur

Track scale

Caboose
track

8" elevation

**THE EK SUB
(N scale)**

Trestle

6¼" elevation

Ramp
track
under

This view shows the joint locations at the corners.

Southbound main

Loco ready tracks

Cut-down
roundhouse

Chemical tank for
water softener

A

Start of 3% grade down
4½" elevation

Old coaling tower

Main

Yard stacks

HAZARD

South

Industry

Oil depot

Start of 3% grade up

Switch tower

Branch track

Railroads usually include the Baltimore & Ohio, Chesapeake & Ohio, Western Maryland, Norfolk & Western, Virginian, and Pennsylvania, while some of the great freelance layouts—

the Virginian & Ohio, Allegheny Midland, Coal Belt, and Cumberland Valley—use similar themes and locales.

Not all Appalachian coal went to Virginia tidewater or Pennsylvania

industry. Some went south to Georgia and the Carolinas. Some set off west, to Cincinnati, Ohio, then north to the Great Lakes or south through Louisville to Tennessee and Alabama.

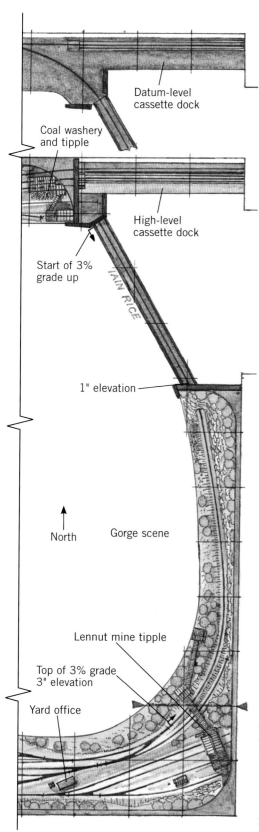

Datum-level
cassette dock

Coal washery
and tipple

High-level
cassette dock

Start of 3%
grade up

MAIN RICE

1" elevation

North

Gorge scene

Lennut mine tipple

Top of 3% grade
3" elevation

Yard office

This last flow was the lifeblood of
one of the great railroads of the South,
the Louisville & Nashville, which
sprawled from Cincinnati to Memphis,
Atlanta, Birmingham, and Mobile,
thence along the Gulf shore to New
Orleans. The L&N tapped the Appalachian coal via a tangle of lines threading the narrow side valleys opening off
the North Fork of the Kentucky River.
This was the East Kentucky section of
the L&N's Corbin Division, known as
the EK Sub.

Stub-end mountain main line
The EK Sub is one tough piece of
railroad, effectively a long, single-track
stub-ended branch leaving the L&N's
Cincinnati-Atlanta main at Patio to
strike southeastward through difficult
hill country to the coalfields of eastern
Kentucky. It's a route rich in sheer-
sided rock cuts, tight tunnels, towering
steel trestles, and snaking curves, running through scenery that's spectacular
and beautiful, especially in fall.

Operationally, the EK Sub had one
long, grinding uphill grade against the
northbound flow of the traffic—the
1 percent Elkatawa Hill, calling for
helpers between Jackson and Yeadon.
EK trains were heavy and frequent,
although—as with most Appalachian
roads—a little lacking in variety: coal,
coal, and more coal.

Fortunately, no railroad rostered a
more eclectic selection of first and second-generation road diesels than the
L&N, which throughout the 1960s and
'70s was perpetually short of motive
power. So odd engines were garnered
here, there, and everywhere from take-
overs, trades, and the demise of other
roads to add to the fleet of mostly Alco
units with which the railroad diesel-
ized. Throughout the 1960s and well
into the '80s the hoppers frequently
tailed outlandish lash-ups of mixed
Alco, GE, and EMD power—often
with units sporting a variety of previ-
ous-owner paint schemes.

In 1972, the L&N joined with the
Seaboard Coast Line and Clinchfield
(plus a few other, smaller railroads
in the South) to form the Family
Lines System. This wasn't a merger
as much as a common marketing alliance coupled to a cooperative working agreement that saw motive power,
equipment, and facilities pooled. So far
as the troubled L&N was concerned,
Family Lines meant an easing of the
capacity crunch and a classy new cor-
porate paint scheme of French gray
with red and yellow stripes—a tad
smarter than the L&N utility all-over
grey then prevailing.

Family Lines operated in this co-
operative alliance mode until 1983,
when the participating railroads for-
mally merged as Seaboard System Corporation, which in turn formed part of
CSX. In 1986, all the railroads owned
by CSX Corporation were grouped
into a new company, CSX Transporta-
tion, and the now-familiar CSX paint
schemes began to replace Family Lines
or Chessie Colors.

The other Hazard ...
If the main line north up to Patio was
the spine of the EK Sub, its heart lay at
Hazard, deep in the Appalachian foothills. Hazard, Ky., has—so far as I'm
aware—nothing whatever to do with
the Hollywood Dukes. Far from it; this
Hazard only sports a single "z" and is a
thoroughly down-to-earth sort of town,
center of a hardworking coal district
with a proud history of good and hard
times shared.

It's the hub from which the coal
branches radiate into the big hills,
winding their way up the mountain
creeks and squeezing through near-ver-
tical-sided gorges.

Branchline mine runs and the workings of the yard at Hazard form the
operational core of this moderate-sized
N scale layout design. The long strings
of hoppers are leavened by local peddler freights bringing in supplies and
serving the few non-coal industries.
The prototype I picked as the main
inspiration for my fictional-but-typical
Romeo Branch was the eight-mile run
out to Harburley and Bulan, but there
are plenty of others to choose from.
The yard at Hazard was, in reality,
pretty cramped. It was located on the
riverbank of the North Fork, with the
town on the other side. A long footbridge linked the two.

In addition to the eight-track classification yard, there was a compact
engine terminal with a nine-stall
roundhouse and, in former years, a
passenger depot. As with most layouts,
though, it's switching that provides the

A Louisville & Nashville coal train begins its climb up a stiff seven-mile-long grade on Duff Mountain in Campbell County, Tennessee in 1977. Alco Century 628 No. 1414 is in the lead. *Art Miller*

main operational interest, so my version of Hazard supposes a few additional lineside industries and facilities to ginger up the local freight. These include a cold-storage distribution warehouse and an oil fuel depot. Even in Perry County, they haven't yet figured out how to run a Chevy on coal!

That said, a possible future for parts of the East Kentucky coalfield lies in methane production and collection, so I've jumped the gun and put in a pilot methane plant at Romeo, calling for gas tank cars. But coal is the main business, and likely to remain so: Current estimates place the untapped reserves of Kentucky coal at 50 to 60 billion tons.

EK trains

EK coal typically rolled in as motley a collection of hoppers and gons as you could imagine. Yes, unit trains of new 100-ton hoppers and new Bethgon coal cars were coming on stream, but a lot of traffic still rolled in older two-bay 55-ton and three-bay 70-ton cars, of a variety of outlines and paint schemes.

Many of the loading facilities were old and restricted in size, unable to handle the big high-sided cars; some coal from the smallest tipples and truck-dumps even still rolled in traditional low-side steel gondolas. And, at this period, every train was still tailed with a bright red or French gray caboose, usually one of the handsome steel bay-window cars built by the L&N at its South Louisville Shops in the 1970s.

L&N/Family Lines and South East Coal Corporation also ran unit coal trains. SEC had its own extensive fleet of cars, finished in an unusual light pea-green paint scheme and carrying SECX reporting marks. You can imagine what the block trains carrying those reporting marks were called. Most SEC traffic rolled behind Family Lines power, but for those occasions when the L&N was clean out of serviceable units, SCE had its own trio of matching pea-green GP38-2s.

L&N clung to steam until 1956, when the last of the big Baldwin M-1 2-8-4s was retired. The road had started to dieselize during the 1940s, buying F units and E6s for passenger work and Alco RS-3s, FAs, and RS-11s for road freight. Pretty soon, though, EMD hood units got in on the act, in the shape of GP7s and GP9s.

Continuing motive power shortages sent L&N to the used locomotive market: ex-Rutland RS-3s joined A-B sets of F2s from the Lehigh & New England, among other dealer-lot bargains. And this mix of off-the-shelf power was spruced up with a few of L&N's home rebuilds: EMD-powered Alco S-1 or an SW9 with an RS-3 hood, anyone?

Second generation power saw EMD GP30s, GP35s, GP38s, GP40s and GE U-boats appearing, while the Monon merger of July 1971 brought a lot more Alcos into the fleet, including the charismatic C-420s. The L&N went six-axle from about 1964—but, as usual, with a mix of this and that: Alco Century 628s mingled with GE

U25Cs and EMD SD35s. The 1979 Family Lines agreement brought a further influx of new and used power onto the railroad: ex-Seaboard Coast Line Alco Centuries, high-horsepower GE U36Cs, and new EMD SD40-2s.

What this means is that for a layout scheme like this, you can buy pretty much any ready-to-run N scale diesel in the almost-certain knowledge that the L&N/Family Lines rostered a few of them somewhere. Although neither the L&N pale gray and yellow or Family Lines French Gray with stripes schemes have ever been popular on models, they have to be among the simplest of paint schemes to apply, calling only for an all-over color coat with the rest of the job done with decals.

Even in the early 1980s, many Family Lines locomotives were running in predecessor paint schemes, so you can also authentically roster units in Seaboard's handsome dark blue or Clinchfield black or gray. All in all, this layout scheme is a diesel collector's delight!

Shared basement, tiered shelves

The site for this moderate-sized bite at the Appalachian coal cake is a small basement area also used as a TV room. It's 12 feet wide by a tad under 16 long, with the entry doorway in one end. These dimensions aren't critical—you could readily adjust the basic scheme for just about any roughly similar-sized site. The premise is that the railroad have minimum impact on other uses of the room, the center of which must be kept clear for furniture. So the EK sub is a compact around-the-walls design using mostly narrow shelves. The widest point, the engine terminal at Hazard, is 20 inches, but the rest of the railroad is 12 inches or less wide.

Along the far end and right-hand side (as seen from the doorway) the layout-supporting shelves are integrated with bookshelves above and below track level. Unlike the Hazard scene, these boards have straight front edges to match this shelving. The track spanning the doorway (just an opening, no door) is a simple lift-out link section to give access when the layout is not in use. The TV and home theater installation lives below Hazard.

This is all straightforward, but the EK does have one less-obvious tweak. Rather than being all mounted at the same level, the boards are tiered, with each one mounted at a different height to the adjoining board. Doing this around three of the walls gains enough extra elevation to allow double-decking along the fourth side, effectively giving a five-sided rectangle footprint.

Starting from a reference point at the north end exit from the staging, the southbound main immediately commences a stiff 3 percent climb over the inclined cross-doorway link, at the end of which it enters the gorge scene board, which is mounted an inch higher than the staging level. Climbing steadily on the same grade up through the gorge, the track has gained another two inches of elevation by the time it reaches the connection with the Hazard board, which is higher than the gorge board by the same amount.

The mainline and yard trackage though Hazard is all on the level at this elevation (three inches above reference). At the south end of the yard, though, the start of the Romeo branch climbs on a curving fill—still at 3 percent—to cross the southbound main at four and a half inches above reference.

The branch then enters the trestle scene board, mounted an inch and a half higher than Hazard, and climbs on over riser-and-spine roadbed to cross the tall steel trestle (still on grade), gaining another three-and-a-half inches by the time it reaches the start of the Romeo board, which is set eight inches above reference. That's just about enough—with shallow (2") framing—to give access clearance for the staging tracks beneath.

This arrangement does pose a few practical problems. Firstly, at the corners, it's necessary to achieve neat and visually acceptable transition between boards mounted at different levels. For reasons I expounded back in Chapter 2, I don't care for steps in the upper fascia within a scene, so I'd opt to keep this at the same level throughout the continuous scene part of the layout—the Gorge, Hazard, and trestle boards—with the mean scene height varying (by a maximum of two inches) accordingly.

A large silo at the Cimarron Coal Co., near Madisonville, Ky., loads hopper cars as a pair of Louisville & Nashville diesels slowly pull the 70-car train under the tipple. *L&N*

Then it's only necessary to provide a step in the lower edge of the layout fascia, as in the first sketch. At the last corner, however, it's necessary not only to raise the upper fascia height (to prevent Romeo from becoming too beetle-browed), but also to make the transition from one deck to two. In this instance, I opt for a total view block to separate the Romeo and Trestle scenes and to incorporate the lower deck.

The other problem is the southbound main track from Hazard, which drops, hidden, back to reference level on a straight ramp track—made in the same way as a link section—located below and to the rear of the trestle scene. The framing of the trestle scene board is set forward slightly to provide the small clearance needed. This arrangement, together with the method used to support the scene board off the shelf brackets, is shown in the cross-section diagram included on the plan. Access to this track, which should rarely be neeeded, is from below.

Other than this slightly awkward hidden section, the trackwork should be quite straightforward. Curves are relatively sweeping, 24 inches or wider. The tightest (18-inch radius and hidden) being the return to staging from the Hazard south end.

The track could be Atlas, Peco, or Micro-Engineering code 55 flex with matching turnouts, which are mostly No. 8 (or Peco "long"). Micro-Engineering's code 40 would be good for the spurs and yard tracks at Romeo. To match the prototype, you'll need plenty of dips and humps, kinks, and doglegs; ballast should be dirty stone on the

main, weeds and coal-waste on the branch. High-iron this ain't!

Cassette cuts

One of the conundrums of all coal-themed model railroads is the old problem of the one-way traffic: coal goes out, empties come in. Short of loading/unloading all those hoppers, how do you ensure that traffic always moves in the right direction? Well, with a continuous-run main as used here, that's easy enough to achieve for through trains. The empties go clockwise around, the coal counter-clockwise. A stub-end branch, though, is much more of a problem. You need to take a cut of empty cars up the branch, and come back down with the same cars, only full.

My solution here is to employ matched cuts of loaded and unloaded hoppers, eight or nine cars long, in this instance. The empties go up the hill, and after run-around and caboose disposal, are pushed through the Romeo tipple onto the yard-long cassette, which can be aligned with either of the tipple tracks. This cassette can then be exchanged for one from the low-level staging containing a like number of loaded cars. You can even go so far as to have matched sets of identical loaded and unloaded hoppers. The "loads" are then drawn out from beneath the tipple a car at a time (to simulate loading) before being spotted, ready to make the trip down to Hazard for switching into longer consists. The low-level staging incorporates a number of cassette berths to handle the other end of this process.

CHAPTER THIRTEEN

The Adirondack & Southern (HO scale)

With several milk cars in tow, New York, Ontario & Western Consolidation No. 307 leads a mixed local train. *H.D. Runey*

This is a somewhat old-fashioned style of layout based on a very old-fashioned style of prototype: a pre-World War II third-rank railroad earning limited revenue, surviving on thrifty management and mostly aged equipment with never a whiff of diesel oil about the property.

The layout concept is old-fashioned in that it's a traditional route design based on a pure freelance fantasy—although one very much inspired by a couple of prototype railroads, the Rutland and the New York, Ontario & Western.

The entirely fictitious Adirondack & Southern inhabits some of the same territory as the NYO&W—basically, the upper left corner of New York State. Unlike the O&W, though, the Adirondack & Southern extends north of the Rochester-Syracuse-Albany corridor. And instead of heading east of south in the direction of New York, the A&S trends to the west, aiming for the Lehigh Valley and the Pennsylvania heartlands.

The northern terminal point of the A&S is Cape Vincent, N.Y., on the shore of the deepwater channel of the St. Lawrence river where it flows out of the eastern extremity of Lake Ontario. Cape Vincent faces the Canadian border at Horne's Point, Wolfe Island, a scant mile away.

This is in my own backyard, so to speak. Many of my family are located on Wolfe, and a cabin at Horne's Point is a regular family retreat. At various times over the past 100 or so years, there have been plans to use Wolfe Island as a stepping stone for a through route into Canada. A bridge or ferry would be used to cross the deep channel and causeways with trestles joining smaller islands to cross the shallow two-and-a-half miles separating the northern shore of Wolfe from Kingston, Ont., and the Canadian National's Toronto-Montreal main line.

Fortunately for the peace of the island, a noted bird sanctuary, nothing has ever come of these proposals. Being a birder myself, my A&S fiction eschews a bridge in favor of a train ferry from Cape Vincent to a deepwater terminal at Colin's Bay, on the northern (Canadian) shore of the lake a few miles west of Kingston—a water distance of about six miles.

Back on dry land, the A&S runs eastward from Cape Vincent to Watertown, where it crosses the NYC Syracuse-Massena line then follows the valley of the Black River east before turning south down through Carthage to Lowville. (Rand McNally, for some unaccountable reason, ascribes this part of the route to the New York Central.) From Lowville, the A&S climbs with the river south to Boonville then a little west up Mill Creek and over a modest

summit at Mineral Springs (elevation 1,100 feet) before descending through the Boonville Gorge, a route shared with the now-defunct Black River Canal (an Erie canal feeder with no fewer than 109 locks in 35 miles).

From the lower end of the gorge, the route turns west to follow the northern shore of Lake Delta, passing north of Rome, N.Y., through New London and thus to Oneida where, of course, it meets the O&W and crosses the NYC Lake Shore route to Buffalo and Chicago. From Oneida, the A&S heads due south over a twisting, switchback alignment through a long, empty stretch of lake-strewn country to Georgetown, Otselic, Pharsalia, and Chenango.

From Chenango Forks, the A&S turns somewhat to the west, crossing over the Delaware, Lackawanna & Western's Binghampton-to-Syracuse line to reach a junction with the Delaware & Hudson and Erie railroads at Johnson City—and a southern outlet into Pennsylvania and New Jersey through Binghampton. From Georgetown, a branch extends a few miles west to DeRuyter and Crains Mills.

Milk, fruit, and manufactures

The section south of Oneida traverses a piece of territory sparsely served by rail. The combination of many hills but few folks hardly had railroad promoters deluging the state legislature with plans and proposals. Like the real O&W, running roughly parallel but a few miles farther to the east, my fictional A&S would have eked out a modest living on what limited through traffic it might have managed to develop between Ontario and the cities of the northeast U.S., together with such farm-based lading as it could pick up on the way. In this neck of the woods that means one thing: milk.

These pastoral rolling hills and green valleys were the home of a great dairying industry, based on the almost-insatiable demands of the big conurbations of New York, northern New Jersey, and Pennsylvania. In dairy country, every town would have its creamery, and the milk cars full of cans or the bulk milk tanks would be

worked smartly south, in the case of the A&S, to the industrial cities of the Lehigh Valley: Allentown, Bethlehem, and Philipsburg.

At this point I must mention a truly wonderful book that gives not only a complete history (with track plans and scale drawings) of the NYO&W but also a detailed rundown of the whole New York dairying industry, complete with more drawings and plans of creameries and information on all the specialized equipment that went with them. Published by Garrigues House, P.O. Box 400, Laurys Station, PA 18059, the *New York, Ontario and Western Railway: Milk Cans, Mixed Trains and Motor Cars* was written by Robert E Mohowski with illustrations by Carl Olson. It is, quite simply, one of the best railroad history books of all time.

The A&S through traffic coming down from Ontario would also be of a perishable nature: fruit and vegetables from the Amherst and Quinte Islands, a rich fruit and produce farming region along the northern shore of Lake Ontario stretching west to Coburg. Going north, boxcars would be laden with manufactured goods of all kinds. This through Canadian traffic would mostly be blocked in through freights, some of them on fast schedules to bring produce fresh to market.

Far from fast, however, would be the peddler freights or mixed trains serving the intermediate towns. Keeping the various creameries supplied with empty, pre-cooled milk cars in good time for the morning and evening milkings would be the operating department's top priority. Milk would roll in dedicated trains or be worked head-end on passenger trains; whatever happened, nothing must delay the dairyman's lifeline.

The passenger operations themselves are pretty well tied to the morning milk traffic or run as leisurely mixed trains during the day—except for one. The A&S's crack varnish, the *Adirondack Mountain Limited,* runs daily—say I—in the summer months, from Allentown to Watertown, conveying a declining handful of vacationers from industrial Pennsylvania to the almost-fashionable mountain retreats

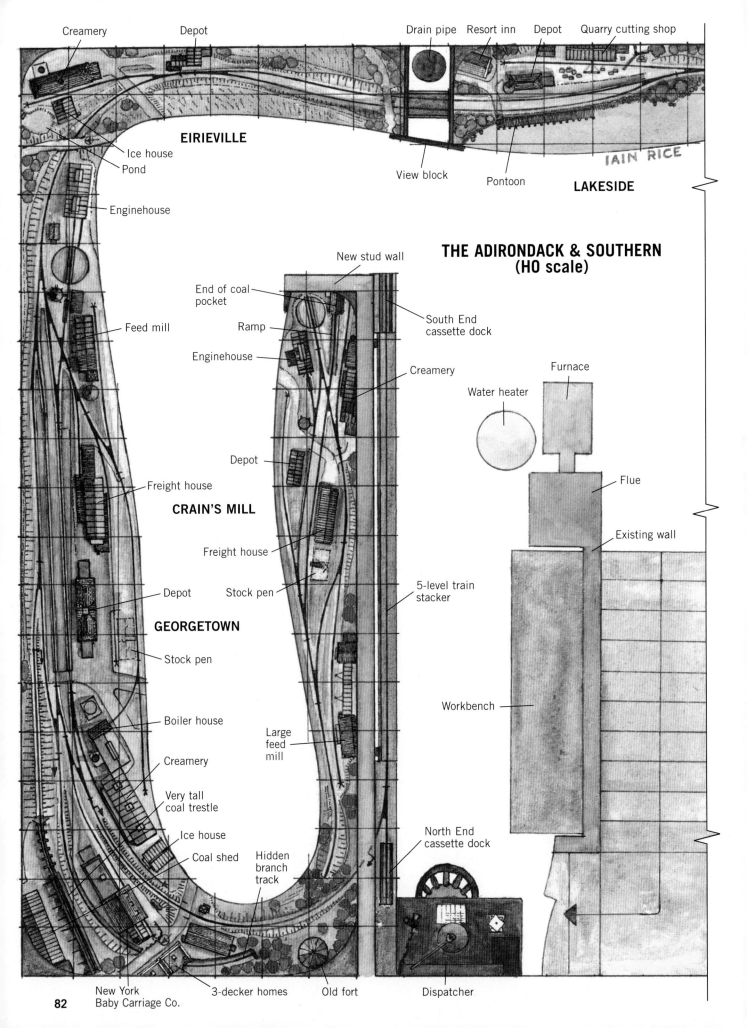

Creamery   Depot   Drain pipe   Resort inn   Depot   Quarry cutting shop

EIRIEVILLE

IAIN RICE

Ice house
Pond

View block   Pontoon   LAKESIDE

Enginehouse

New stud wall

THE ADIRONDACK & SOUTHERN
(HO scale)

End of coal
pocket

Ramp

South End
cassette dock

Enginehouse

Feed mill

Creamery

Water heater   Furnace

Depot

Freight house

Flue

CRAIN'S MILL

Existing wall

Freight house

Depot

5-level train
stacker

Stock pen

GEORGETOWN

Workbench

Stock pen

Large
feed
mill

Boiler house

Creamery

Very tall
coal trestle

North End
cassette dock

Ice house

Coal shed

Hidden
branch
track

New York
Baby Carriage Co.   3-decker homes   Old fort   Dispatcher

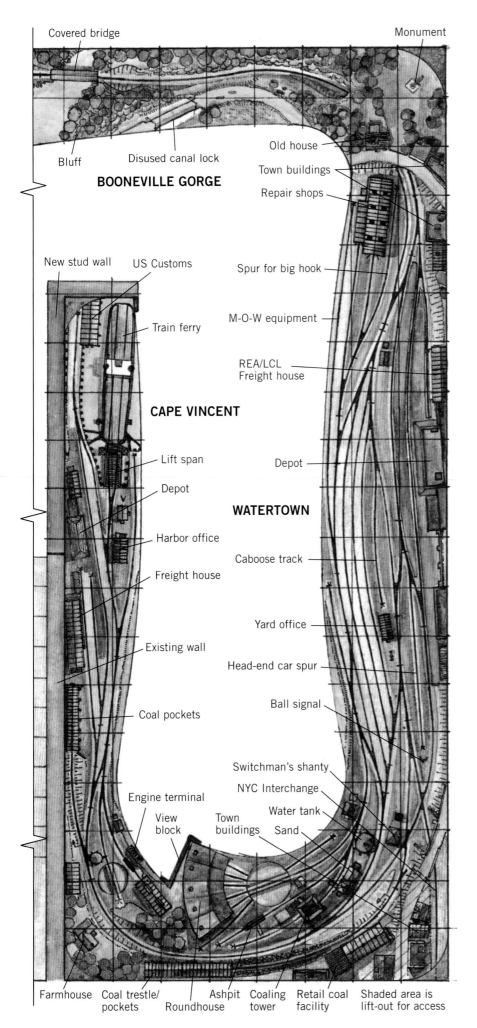

Covered bridge

Monument

Old house

Town buildings

Repair shops

BOONEVILLE GORGE

Bluff

Disused canal lock

New stud wall

US Customs

Spur for big hook

M-O-W equipment

Train ferry

REA/LCL
Freight house

CAPE VINCENT

Lift span

Depot

Depot

Harbor office

WATERTOWN

Freight house

Caboose track

Existing wall

Yard office

Head-end car spur

Coal pockets

Ball signal

Switchman's shanty

NYC Interchange

Engine terminal

Water tank

View
block

Town
buildings

Sand

Farmhouse

Coal trestle/
pockets

Ashpit

Coaling
tower

Retail coal
facility

Shaded area is
lift-out for access

Roundhouse

in the western hills of the Adirondack range, or to yachting havens on the Ontario lakeshore.

An all-round model railroad

The fiction of the Adirondack & Southern outlined above has, of course, been carefully contrived to allow a model railroad featuring a little bit of everything.

Like its twin inspirations, the O&W and the Rutland, the A&S would roster a modest but somewhat mixed selection of locomotives, a handful of passenger equipment (including older wooden-bodied cars for the local and mixed runs and a half-dozen steel heavyweights for the *Adirondack Mountain Limited),* the all-important fleet of milk cars, and a few hundred assorted freight cars.

Privately owned milk cars in colorful paint schemes would also figure in its trains, while much of the through freight would ride in foreign-road equipment.

Small though the A&S may be, frugality and enterprise have kept it a solvent enterprise, characterized by the signature fast produce train, the *Ontario Arrow,* with its smart consist of specially painted ventilated all-steel boxcars and reefers. It's not dissimilar to the *Whippet* premium express service offered by the Rutland.

Like many American railroads, the A&S would have been built on the cheap, with minimal earthworks and civil engineering. The theory was that the route would be upgraded once the revenue started to roll in. For the A&S, as for many similar lines, the revenue never quite got to the level anticipated, so the opportunities for improvement were limited. Steel bridges or fills might replace timber trestles. Grades or curves might be eased here and there, and heavier rails and stone (rather than dirt) ballast give a better line and a smoother ride.

But the big money for extensions, branch lines, cut-offs, tunnels, and re-alignments along easier grading never figured in the account books, leaving a legacy of operating difficulties to challenge the traffic department. Stations and other structures were never rebuilt, modern dispatching systems went untried, and locomotives and cars stayed in service long after similar equipment vanished from richer roads.

No matter; for a comfortable half-century—say, 1890 to around 1940—the A&S made a modest living at the bottom of the railroad big league. Some years it was a bona fide Class 2, other years not quite. If there wasn't money for much in the way of new infrastructure and equipment, there was enough to keep the existing fabric of the railroad in fair order. The A&S was poor but proud, old but not shabby.

And, like its prototype inspirations, the A&S developed a distinctive character, a railroad unmistakably different from the big players with which it was surrounded. Had it existed, I'm sure Messrs. Beebe and Clegg, Hastings, and scores of other dedicated railfans would have paid it a visit.

Landscape setting, scenic breaks and structures

The A&S is conceived to be a visually pleasing layout, set in beautiful and modelable scenery ranging from the relatively mountainous topography of the Adirondack Division (north of Oneida) to the rolling, wooded hillsides and lush valleys of Madison, Chenango, and Broome counties on the southern (Georgetown) division. So far as the model goes, this attractive landscape is represented in a series of scenes which, while not truly continuous, do keep a strict sense of direction, orientation, and correct order.

In keeping with the traditional form of this design, I've largely eschewed artificial picture frame view blocks to separate the various scenes, relying instead on natural features (mostly hills and trees) to act as demarcations. The exceptions are between Cape Vincent and Watertown, and at the joint between the "north" and "south" ends of the layout where the line negotiates a drain pipe on the wall. A wide view block here hides both pipe and the missing 50-odd miles of railroad.

So, we have pair of fair-sized scenes encompassing Cape Vincent and Watertown (with the main yard and shops), followed by a narrow slice of the Adirondack Division section through the Boonville Gorge and along the shore of Lake Delta, which last forms a "greet scene" at the foot of the basement stairs. Now comes the black hole around the drain pipe, where a large stretch of railroad—including Oneida—is ignored, and the model takes up the trail again well to the south with the second main scene, featuring Georgetown Junction and the branch to Crains Mills. South of Georgetown, the main line runs into staging, in the form of a five-deck train stacker.

This being a shelf layout supported off the wall on gallows brackets, most of the scenes are relatively shallow front-to-back, which means that the scenic success of the model is going to depend to a large extent on the backdrop. Fortunately, the open rolling hills of Chenango county and the slightly steeper and heavily forested Western Adirondacks are a relatively simple subject for the backdrop painter, with no tricky problems of perspective and very few structures to represent.

Backdrop apart, as a modeling proposition we're talking mostly the earthworks of the actual railroad, pretty much contained within the boundary fences. The rest is field edges and occasional trees on the "southern" scenes and rock cuts, with heavy lineside vegetation and plenty of trees in the mountains.

Any layout scheme centered on this region is going to need a selection of attractive signature structures. Upper New York is covered bridge and mansard-barn country, so examples of these characteristic pieces of functional design are featured amid the hills, along with neatly fenced or walled field boundaries. But it's alongside the railroad that we find the most important signatures: coal pockets and creameries.

Coal pockets are ramped, elevated tracks, usually timber trestle structures, to facilitate the use of bottom-drop gondolas. Many were roofed in against the winter snow. The creameries were often elegant pagoda-roofed buildings, accompanied by windowless ice houses to store the winter harvest of 200-lb ice-cakes needed to cool the milk at the creamery. There are three creameries and two ice houses on the A&S.

Divided basement

The site for the Adirondack & Southern is the basement area of a smaller suburban home, roughly 20 feet square (actually 19 x 23) with the staircase dropping down slightly off-center of the 23-foot axis and the furnace and flue in the middle of the floor area off to one side. Fortunately, the relatively small size of the basement and the solid walls either side of the stairway keep the floor beams short, which in turn means that there are no support posts to get in the way. The only impediment is a large-diameter drain pipe on the rear wall.

The A&S is conceived as a shelf layout, but of course to support shelves you need walls. From which it follows that the more walls there are, the more shelves you can have and the longer the length of run that can be accommodated.

The key to getting the run needed for the A&S concept proved to be to not only make as much use as possible of the existing masonry basement walls (including those either side of the stairs), but also to introduce some additional partition walls, simply built as studs covered with drywall. These stud additions comprise a short extension to one staircase wall, with a further parallel wall dividing the main basement space. This results in a usable wall length of something over 120 feet, compared to about 85 feet without the extra walls.

These walls divide the basement into three distinct areas, plus the staircase. There are two main bays along the outer walls (eight and six feet wide respectively and running the full width of the basement) together with a narrow passage bay four and five feet wide and 15 feet deep. This last is indeed a passage as it gives access to the electrical cabinet and gas supply stop-valve, as well as a drain cover located beneath the stairs.

Maximum route, minimum space

In keeping with its traditional subject, the A&S also takes a traditional approach to track planning, with no offstage trickery and a pretty high density. The design was intended from the outset to operate under traditional telegraph-and-train-order control with a dispatcher. Relating to the site, the two large bays were the obvious homes for the main focal points, Cape Vincent–Watertown and Georgetown; these are linked by the long, narrow open line over Mineral Springs summit and along the shore of Delta Lake.

The narrow passage area around the boiler flue houses the south-end staging on the new stud wall. The other face of this supports the branch terminal, Crains Mills. Also shoehorned into this area are a workbench and storage, while at the far end—tucked neatly away under the stairs—sits the dispatcher's desk.

The A&S is a "sincere" walkaround end-to-end design in which the main objective was to get as long a main line as possible, linking a number of different towns and facilities and providing just enough distance between them for operational purposes and visual separation.

There are just three main interest centers and one subsidiary: the dock, yard, and ferry terminal at Cape Vincent; the railroad's northern (Adirondack) division-point yard and shops at Watertown, where the A&S interchanges with the NYC; and the yard, engine terminal, and junction at Georgetown, division point for the south. The subsidiary interest comes from the branch stub terminal at Crain's Mills.

Cape Vincent is a waterside facility, and the method of operation for the train ferry is similar to that described for car floats on the Elm Point scheme earlier in the book. Cape Vincent also features a coal depot and a single-stall enginehouse for the resident switcher; cars for the ferry are worked as short cuts from Watertown Yard. (In reality, Cape Vincent and Watertown are only a few miles apart.)

Watertown itself, as befits the road's headquarters, has a yard, interchange track with the NYC, a LCL/mail and express freight house, the repair shops, a coal yard and, of course, the engine terminal with five-stall roundhouse. Alongside the shop building are spurs for the road's "big hook," maintenance-of-way, and snow-fighting equipment. It's all business—mostly track, very little scenery.

South of Watertown, I kept the route free of major interest centers, preferring instead to concentrate on exploiting the scenic opportunities. So we have the Booneville Gorge, complete with a derelict lock of the Black River Canal, followed by a pair of simple wayside stations. A station flanks either side of the drain pipe that divides the north and south scenes.

These are: Lakeside, a vacation stop serving Delta Lake and featuring a resort inn, boat pontoon, and covered bridge. There's also a spur serving a small bluestone quarry. And Erieville, inspired by Northfield on the O&W, dressed up by adding a creamery. An unusual feature of these two stations is the common passing siding that starts in one scene and carries through the divide into the other. For timetable purposes, this siding is deemed to be in Erieville for trains headed south or at Lakeside for northbounds. This keeps the dispatcher on his toes.

Georgetown yard is inspired by Walton on the O&W. It features a substantial creamery with ice house, a large set of coal pockets, a stockyard, a solitary manufacturing industry, a freight house, and a feed mill, together with a three-stall enginehouse and turntable. (The real Walton did without a turntable as there was a wye, but Georgetown doesn't have space for this luxury.) At the south end is the junction for the branch to Crain's Mill.

To keep the geographic orientation correct—Crain's Mill is actually west of the main line, whereas the model positions it to the east—this branch takes off in the right direction, but promptly dives downhill on a hidden alignment as the main line climbs. The branch can then pass unseen beneath the main to run into the modeled terminus of Crain's Mill—where there is another creamery, a large feed mill, stock ramps, a coal depot, and a small engine facility with turntable. The very visible 3 percent grade on the southbound main

line as it leaves Georgetown represents the start of the big climb on the southern section of the A&S, which, as with the O&W north of Walton, is a helper district. These are the only grades on the layout.

Operation

The layout is designed around a normal minimum crew of five operators—two mainline engineers, two yardmasters and a dispatcher, who also looks after the south end staging/fiddle yard. Solo operation would be possible if the pace was kept leisurely enough, while a dozen or so operators could find gainful employment if the layout was operated intensively. The working timetable would be dominated by the milk trains, the hotshot through freights down from Canada, and the daily run of the *Adirondack Mountain Limited*. Serving the creameries would also call for frequent extra trains. Whatever happens, the milk must never be kept waiting.

The south-end mainline staging is set up to handle trains with helper engines, using cassettes at either end of the eight-and-a-half foot train-stacker to accommodate the locomotives. The lead engine runs right through the stacker onto the "south end" cassette, with an uncoupling magnet at the end of the stacker to part it from the train. The helper engine can, after a suitable pause, either be run back light to Georgetown, or it can be shunted onto a cassette via the north end "dock" above the dispatcher's desk.

Cassettes can be switched and turned end-for-end to release engines and ready them for placing at the head of a northbound train using the north-end dock. Spare locomotives would be stored in cassettes on shelves above the north-end cassette dock. All this should keep the dispatcher busy when he's not pushing paper.

Equipment

It probably hasn't escaped your notice that there has never been a better time to model a steam-era freelance railroad like this, as pretty much everything you need is readily available out there for moderate prices. Motive power couldn't be more straightforward (unless you're

Rutland 4-8-2 No. 93 works her way south out of Rutland, Vt., with the Troy, N.Y.-bound section of the Green Mountain Flyer. At Troy, the coaches will proceed to New York City behind New York Central power. The scene is from September 1951. *John Pickett*

seduced by O&W-style Camelbacks): Bachmann's charismatic Ten-Wheeler (high-boiler version) and 2-8-0 Consolidation are ideal backbone power for the over-the-road passenger, milk, and road freight trains. A handful of USRA 2-8-2s handle the through manifest runs to Canada, and a USRA light Mountain could work the *Mountain Limited.*

The branch line from Georgetown to Crains Mills could keep a Bachmann modern 4-4-0 or IHC Mogul employed, maybe filling in with yard work at Georgetown and the odd extra trip on the main. Yard work at Watertown and Cape Vincent would call for a switcher or two—USRA 0-6-0s from Proto would fit the bill nicely. Last call on the motive power shopping list (and the only non-steam items) would be a couple of gas-electric combination cars for minor passenger operations between the milk runs, following once again in the footsteps of the O&W.

Rolling stock is likewise pretty straightforward, mostly off the shelf ready to roll. The main exception is wooden-bodied passenger cars, not yet available in mass-produced plastic. There have been brass models and the lovely old LaBelle wood car kits, but probably the best bet will be resin kits from the likes of Funaro & Camarlengo, which lists a complete selection of genuine O&W cars at moderate

cost. Resin kits are not that hard to build using modern CA adhesives, and they have a similar degree of relief and detailing to plastic cars.

Walthers and IHC both list a good selection of classic steel heavyweights for the *Mountain Limited,* while if you want to emulate the O&W and tail-up your crack varnish with an observation car, then F&C can sell you a kit for the genuine item.

Freight cars are even more straightforward, as roads like the A&S would mostly have bought standard AAR-design equipment from the big car-makers. Boxcars would be mostly older outside-braced wood types in the 1930s, with only a smattering of newer all-steel cars in home-road paint. But, of course, just about anything could show up in interchange service. One feature (pinched from the O&W) is the use of steel-framed wood-side bottom-drop gons for the coal traffic. A lot of the small creameries—most of which used coal to fire their boilers—simply had a gon spotted handy to the boiler-house; the coal was shovelled straight out of the car right into the furnace.

Other traffic includes livestock, lumber, and forest products, high-grade quarried stone, animal feeds, seeds, fertilizers, machinery, and fuel oils. Thus stock cars, flats, more gons, and tank cars would also figure. The

few cabooses would likewise be standard designs, although the O&W was a great user of four-wheel bobbers, and one or two might linger about the property if the A&S followed suit.

Which leaves the milk cars, key equipment for the road. They carried milk and cream in cans, although later cars used bulk milk tanks inside the car body. Early wood cars looked like classic express reefers, but did not have ice bunkers. The car's insulation kept the milk cool for its relatively short run to the big city. There was considerable variety in design and detail, with the 50-foot wood-sheathed "billboard" cars on Pullman or Commonwealth trucks and steel 40-foot cars on express trucks being the most typical.

Athearn has listed the former type and InterMountain the latter. Many of the more specialized or oddball cars figure in Funaro & Camerlengo's resin kit line. The company also makes the distinctive whaleback milk tank cars introduced in the late 1920s. For the most part, the "can cars" were owned by the railroads, while the cars with internal tanks were owned by the General American Pfaudler Corporation or General American Refrigerator Express and leased by the big dairy combines—Borden, Dairymen's League, Hood's, and Sheffield Farms.

About the author

Iain Rice is a retired firefighter who earns his living designing, custom building, lecturing, and writing about model railroads both in the U.S. and in Europe. His byline has appeared on 20 modeling book titles and more than 350 feature articles for UK, U.S., and European magazines—including regular contributions to *Model Railroader* and *Model Railroad Planning*. He was recently appointed a contributing editor to the Layout Design SIG's authoritative *Layout Design Journal*. A small-layout man from inclination as much as as necessity, Iain currently has four compact fine scale model railroads of his own, all in shelf format: Two British-prototype in 4mm/1ft scale, a Dutch "lokaalspoor," and a Maine Central branchline terminal in HO. All these models are exhibited regularly at UK and European train shows and meets.

Formerly married with two daughters, most of Iain's family live on Wolfe Island, Ontario, where he spends as much time as he can. But his current home is an historic 200-year-old stone cottage in the far west of England—an on-going restoration project between his frequent travels and a home base for his younger daughter Bryony, an aid worker currently serving in Cambodia. Aside from railroads, Iain's other interests include hiking the wild hill-country on his doorstep, gardening, conservation work and researching local history—on which he also writes.

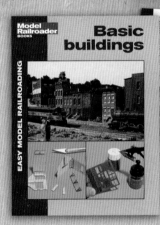

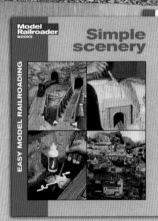

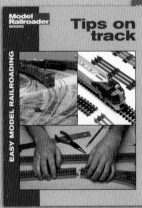
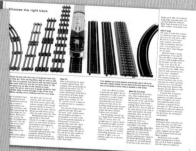

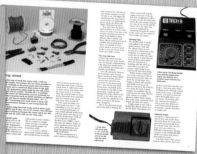